Praise for *Someday This Will Fit:*

This delightful collection is filled with gemlike assertions, wit, and an unflinching eye that captures the truth of what it means to be human. I loved this book, which does double-duty as a perfect vacation read.

—**KIM DANA KUPPERMAN**
author of *Six Thousand Miles to Home*
and *The Last of Her: A Forensic Memoir*

"Happiness consists more in small conveniences or pleasures that occur every day, than in great pieces of good fortune that happen but seldom," Ben Franklin wrote to a friend. Franklin would enjoy visiting Joan Silverman. Her deftly written vignettes are like spending time with a good neighbor, one who is observant, funny, and a little chatty, one who knows the happiness of finding the perfect small spoon for a yogurt cup.

—**HOWARD MANSFIELD**
author of *The Habit of Turning the World Upside Down*

Joan Silverman's essays remind us of the wonders of the everyday. A delight to read!

—**BERND HEINRICH**
author of *Summer World* and *Mind of the Raven*

Joan Silverman's clear-eyed narrative mines small daily details for larger lessons about everything from music to mortality. With sharp observations and wry humor, Silverman delivers wise and timely home truths.

—**ELIZABETH SEARLE**
author of *A Four-Sided Bed* and *Tonya & Nancy: The Rock Opera*

SOMEDAY
THIS WILL FIT

Linked Essays, Meditations
& Other Midlife Follies

Joan Silverman

To Sven —
Thanks very much for your
endorsement. A huge help in this
strange adventure!

Joan

BAUHAN PUBLISHING
PETERBOROUGH, NEW HAMPSHIRE
2019

ISBN: 978-0-87233-299-7

Library of Congress Cataloging-in-Publication Data:
LCCN 2019030065 (print)
LC record available at https://lccn.loc.gov/2019030065

Joan Silverman can be reached through her website
www.joansilverman.com

Book design by Kirsty Anderson
Text set in Michael Harvey's Mentor Pro and Strayhorn
Cover design by Henry James
Illustration of Joan Silverman by Nancy Januzzi (www.nancyjanuzzi.com)

BAUHAN
PUBLISHING LLC
PO BOX 117 PETERBOROUGH NEW HAMPSHIRE 03458
603-567-4430
WWW.BAUHANPUBLISHING.COM
Follow us on Facebook and Twitter – @bauhanpub

Manufactured in the United States of America

To my mother

CONTENTS

INTRODUCTION

A friend recently sent me a birthday gift, a book that's long on photos, short on text.

Inside a handwritten note said: "I thought you might enjoy this because of how few words it has!"

An odd inscription to send to a writer, perhaps, except that it wasn't. Long before our collective attention span rivaled that of a gnat, I was a fan of short, distilled formats. I preferred "shorts" in movies, music, books, and elsewhere.

I've felt that way as a writer, too. As a young journalist at Boston's *Real Paper*, I relished the opportunity to write short reviews of any and everything—ice cream and crêpes, dry cleaners and car mechanics. Composing blurbs was good training for fledgling writers who tend to be enthralled with the sound of their own voice.

Little did anyone know, back in the late '70s, that blurbs were a predigital forebear of Twitter—forty characters, with a bit more flesh.

Since those early days, writing gave me the chance to indulge my curiosity. I wrote profiles, features, and reviews for publications including *The Boston Globe, Boston Phoenix*, and *Boston Magazine*. For several years, I wrote about botanists and plant breeders who helped shape the American garden. An article that I wrote for *Horticulture* led to a call from an editor at the *Chicago Tribune*. That set me on a new path of building relationships with editors at periodicals coast to coast. As a freelancer, I could write for newspapers in Dallas, Chicago, or L.A., which seemed nearly exotic before the internet.

Later I went on to write op-eds and essays, many of which appeared in publications around the country. Although I was new to this genre, there was much to write about: My mother had recently died, and my father, newly widowed, was showing signs of dementia. I had just moved and my life was in flux. Not to mention that technology was starting to eclipse old-fashioned human contact and American culture was in the midst of sweeping, millennial change. If there was an ongoing theme to my columns, it was the stuff of daily life. I quickly discovered that first-person writing needn't be a forum for navel-gazing; it's a point of view, not a mirror. Inevitably my stories went beyond the personal—they reflected the lives of readers, as well.

Recently, sorting through the pieces that I wrote over the last couple of decades, I found that many of their themes and questions were as on point today as when they were first published.

Who gets bragging rights to a family's legendary pie recipe?

What is it about an old, threadbare dictionary that inspires loyalty?

Why do we give our friends leeway in their attitudes, yet politicians are "flip-floppers" if they change their minds?

And how do we cope with a dying parent?

I also realized that the hundreds of first-person pieces I'd written over the years formed a larger story that had yet to be told. I began to sift through these pieces, gathering those with common threads and interweaving them into a collection of linked essays. What emerges is a tapestry of daily life in all its richness, complexity, and humor.

AUTHOR'S NOTE

The essays in this collection were culled from hundreds that I wrote over the last two decades.

Some of them first ran as op-eds, others as guest columns, in various newspapers. I'm grateful to the editors who published these pieces, especially those in other parts of the country where space for outsiders was always in short supply. They made room for New England-based stories that were equally at home elsewhere.

Each of the vignettes in this book previously appeared, in slightly different form, in one or more of the following publications: *The American Reporter, Atlanta Journal-Constitution, Christian Science Monitor, Dallas Morning News, Florida Times-Union, Fort Worth Star-Telegram, Houston Chronicle, Journal of Commerce, Journal Tribune, Los Angeles Daily News, MetroWest Daily News, National Book Review, Oregonian, Pittsburgh Post-Gazette, Plain Dealer, Portland Press Herald / Maine Sunday Telegram, Providence Journal, St. Petersburg Times, Spokesman-Review,* and *Toledo Blade.*

In combination, the essays in this book form an original work that has not appeared previously in any format. Note that certain names and details have been changed to protect people's privacy.

CHAPTER ONE: AT HOME

I arrived home late one night from a trip, dumped my suitcase in the hall, and turned on the lights. I noticed that the kitchen seemed a bit dim, so I grabbed a couple of fresh bulbs from the cabinet. I continued my rounds, checking the mail, singling out a desperate fern for immediate watering.

As I re-entered the kitchen, I noted that the light looked strangely murky—not the usual bright white, but a clouded parchment. I took out the stepladder and climbed up. As I lowered the fixture from the ceiling, a rush of cold, brownish, insulation-filled water came pouring down.

I went up to the attic to trace the source of the problem. There I found damp rafters, damp insulation, the trail of water that had descended into my kitchen.

Next day, I called the electrician and roofer, and began a new chapter in The Joys of Old House Ownership. True, I'd lived in this century-old Colonial for six years. I had already encountered the basic sink backups, basement floods, and frozen pipes. But I was unprepared for this latest plot detail.

Rule Number One: Old houses have stories to tell, and they are rarely short stories. More often, they're long, winding sagas with a rotating cast of characters—plumbers, electricians, and assorted other players.

"We can aim for the simple, cost-effective solution and hope that it works," the roofer proclaimed.

Not a vote of confidence, exactly, but a sensible approach. We would start with Band-Aids, and hope to avert the need for surgery. The roofer would reseal the edges of the skylight, which was the likely culprit. An architect-friend advised that I proceed with the plan.

The ladders went up, the skylight was sealed, the ladders came down.

Soon after, I walked into the kitchen one rainy morning to be greeted by a puddle in the middle of the floor. I stationed two buckets under the offending leaks and picked up the phone.

"Quick-and-dirty didn't work," I said to the roofer. "What next?"

We reviewed the possibilities; I consulted again with my architect-friend.

The next plan involved more extensive and costly repairs. One hot summer day, the roofer and his two assistants set up scaffolding on the roof where they spent the afternoon hammering away. A five-year warranty accompanied the work. I paid the bill and waited for a strong, wind-driven rain before concluding that the trouble was over.

It wasn't.

Rule Number Two: Roof leaks are one of the more tenacious house problems. They're hard to trace and hard to stop.

True, there were now only ounces of water where there had been pints and quarts. We had found a treatment, but still no cure. The roofer returned a third and a fourth time for yet more remedial work.

Meanwhile, my kitchen went many months looking like a construction site. The electrician installed a "pigtail," a naked light bulb that hung from a socket in the center of the ceiling. Surrounding the socket were cracks in the ceiling plaster, like waterlogged veins, that extended several feet in every direction.

Rule Number Three: There are simple problems and complicated ones. An old house is, by definition, a complicated one. It's like the hypochondriac who has real ailments, to boot. If it's not one thing, it's surely another.

Several months later, with the roof leak finally resolved, the electrician returned to install new ceiling fixtures. He pulled down the pigtail, and put up a simple, white, half-round glass unit. He repeated this process several feet away, where a second fixture, untouched by the leak, had been supplying a more finished source of light.

"We've run into a problem," he called out from his ladder.

Seems that the second light contained old, cracked, potentially hazardous wiring. He offered to install a new pigtail, where there had been no previous trouble. And he'd return next week to rewire the second light—that is, to resolve a problem I didn't know I had.

Rule Number Four: Old houses have character that new houses lack. That's both the party line and the simple truth. Equally true is that character, whether in people or property, often comes at great expense.

❧ ❧

Benjamin Franklin had the right idea, though he stopped short. Among the certain things in life, rudeness must surely rank alongside death and taxes.

My property tax bill arrived with evidence of this. Inside, a notice entitled "Winter Storm Information" offered this bit of advice: "Do not put snow on others' property. If you plow your driveway, do not push snow across the street onto neighbor's walk."

Excuse me?

Or consider this city ordinance, lower on the page: "Do not block pedestrian passage on a sidewalk by placing snow or ice in the way."

Apparently, some of us have failed Civics 101, not to mention the rudiments of good manners. Granted, piles of snow can be a huge headache. Few of us have enough land to make snow removal a cinch. Some people actually have to think about where to put the offending white stuff. Unless, of course, you just deposit it on a neighbor's lot.

But since when did this become a solution?

True, your neighbor's lot might solve one problem, but surely it would set off another. The neighbor might assume that your little snow-gift was a hostile act—at the least, inconsiderate.

"Where else was I supposed to put it?" you might ask rhetorically.

Such uncivil logic, however, is purely one-sided. It moves the problem without removing it. While this may be a seasonal issue, it doesn't end in April. It merely changes form.

If you've ever watched someone use a leaf blower, you've probably seen one of two things: leaves being blown into bags, or strewn all over the adjacent (read: neighbor's) lot.

The notion that leaves belong on someone else's property, and that one might actually pay to displace them there, is a remarkable leap of imagination. It's one thing for nature to run its course—a little wind picks up, a few leaves relocate. But what would possess one to, how shall we say, "expedite" the process?

How different is that, really, from dumping trash on a neighbor's lawn?

Not very, if you're the recipient.

Leaves, like snow, are equal opportunity squatters: they land, indifferent to place or welcome. Squatters may have certain rights—but neighbors, you'll find, have expectations.

✼ ✿ ✼

Some winters just refuse to quit. Tenacity may be a virtue in humans, but few of us admire it as a meteorological trait. And it can drive some people, like my friend Judy, to extremes. Fed up with the persistent whiteness and unrelenting cold of last winter, she finally succumbed. In a moment of weakness, this die-hard gardener who abhors fakery in all its forms bought herself silk flowers.

Winter had claimed yet another casualty—the elitism of the garden snob.

Personally, I disagree with Judy on this front. I'm more of a situational gardener. While Mother Nature may be the undisputed source of greenery, heavy weather tends to cramp her style. That's when I'm more than willing to take liberties—when bleakness rules the landscape and sanity needs to prevail.

So, there I was last week at a home furnishings store, toying with a tray of faux plants. By that, I mean bending their branches, tipping petals this way or that, and otherwise manipulating their make-believe parts.

Artificial plants have become a virtual Gumby garden of movable limbs. Nor are all specimens of a given type identical. The fake ferns on the table had different shapes, as they would in nature. Ditto for the wonderfully complex hydrangeas with their multicolored petals and variously sized leaves. Other wannabes had their share of browned-out stems, not unlike what you'd find in an actual garden.

I confess that I bought one of these imposters. At home, I plunked it in the most unnatural spot—my desk, where no self-respecting plant has ever survived. This one will surely outdo its predecessors.

Then yesterday, while grocery shopping, I spotted a live rendition of my copycat plant. It was perfectly formed and dark green throughout—not a blemish to be found. If anything, it looked less real and more suspect than my stand-in at home. Had the two specimens been side-by-side, my knockoff would handily have won the prize for street cred.

What's wrong with this picture?

In the old days, artificial plants were so blatantly cheesy that comparisons were beside the point. Too often their style or materials barely replicated more than a hint of the real thing. Today, by contrast, some of the copies are so good that you have to get up close and personal to know for sure. In a strange turn of events, it's sometimes the live plants that look more aspirational, like they're trying too hard to please.

Now that April is here, our winter ploys can be retired for the year. Thankfully, real gardens—with real flowers for cutting—will soon take their place.

If you love books, you've probably noticed their tendency to multiply, to crop up everywhere in your home. On a bench, by the bedside, on tables—anywhere a chunk of real estate allows. At first you don't mind the little stacks of books rising out of the floor; they're actually quaint along the side of a stair. But quaintness finally gives way to overcrowding, and all of you need more space. So it was in my house not that long ago.

While visiting last year, a friend sized up the problem and the solution. She pointed to a trio of windows in my den, under which built-in shelving would handily absorb my stray books. Sometimes it takes an outsider's eye to see what's right under your nose.

A couple of months later, my new bookcase arrived. Suddenly I was reclaiming old surfaces, sorting and shelving, adding sense to the sensibility of having things in their place.

Nor were these the only rewards. Rows of books on shelves impart an air of depth and history, as if the aggregate of all those words, and the stories they tell, add up to a universe, of sorts. Whether or not such loftiness pertains, the basic concept applies: Books on shelves denote tangible substance in an increasingly virtual world.

My new bookcase has that solid, feet-on-the-ground aspect, if not the loftiness, going for it. It also has considerable spine—literally, hundreds of spines of books in varying shapes, sizes, colors, and textures. Over time, I've come to view those books, standing upright with their perfect posture, as an army of sorts, defending against, well, their disappearance.

Visit the homes of people under, say, thirty, and the shelves often tell a different story. They're filled with discs, not books, and it's a one-size-fits-all proposition. More often than not, a flat-screen TV dominates the main room, and nowhere can a comfy chair be found, with a suitable lamp, for old-fashioned reading.

I know, I know. Things change, books now live on e-readers and in the cloud, and I should evolve with the times. In fact, I have, which may explain my ambivalence. Most of my reading now takes place on a tablet or laptop—I admit my collusion in this regard.

No wonder there's an entire industry that sells books in bulk to interior decorators. If one lacks hardcovers or paperbacks that have been read, lived in, and pored over, they can simply be acquired en masse, their character and résumé assumed.

If I were a young person setting up house today, I might be looking to those books-in-bulk outfits for help. Kindles, Nooks, and other tablets may open up entire worlds. But downloads, even of literature, will never convey the sensory pleasures of living in the company of books.

❧ ❧

When we moved into our house, I was the model of efficiency. I had a master list that assigned furniture to designated rooms, colored labels that directed each box to its proper home. The plan was simple: everything in its place. Not that this was realistic, but it was an antidote to the stress of relocating.

Moving is a worrisome thing. We go from what's familiar and known to a state of uncertainty. Our lives are recast into boxes, dozens of them, that elude any real control. In transit, we aim for an accurate inventory, and hope for the best.

To prepare for the new place, we envision all sorts of things. We imagine the life that might be lived there, the activities that will take place. We ask the mover to locate the desk away from the window so that we're not distracted by the view; or in front of the window, specifically to savor the view. We know certain things about ourselves, about the new space, and we take our best guess.

So much for fantasy.

Seven years of living in this house is clear evidence that real life messes things up.

It's difficult to account for the process by which this messiness occurs—it happens slowly and incrementally, so the process is barely perceptible. Then one day you realize that you can't recall having seen a particular surface in years, it's been buried so long.

It's hard to anticipate which room, or table, or closet will become the de facto cemetery in one's house, the permanent resting ground for things that have no other place. But it's unmistakable when it happens. The illusion is that these displaced items, as yet unaffiliated, are waiting for a proper home—that space will turn up elsewhere to relieve the overcrowding.

For me, the pantry became that cemetery.

At an earlier stage, my pantry actually functioned as a pantry. It stored food and cooking equipment, kitchen paraphernalia of all sorts. But over the years, as new and unrelated items started to mingle with the old, the bond between kitchen and pantry was broken. My pantry had become a potter's field where no unnamed thing was turned away. As a result, it became impossible to find the many named things that were also buried there.

Serious corrective measures were needed.

The real question was how to solve the pantry problem without creating other problems. The answer was to be ruthless. Understand that everything you've saved elicits some memory or emotion, and this is no time to displace feelings from one room to the next. If something is worthless in the pantry, its fortunes won't improve somewhere else. Dump it. The questions were hard-nosed and practical: what to chuck, what to save, where to put it.

In all, reconstructing the pantry took about twelve hours. I rethought how I used the space, which items I used at all, and which things had sat idly for years. I was beyond the new-house fantasies I once harbored—those addle-brained notions of how one's life or habits might change in a new setting.

When we move, what changes most are the four walls that surround us. Though we don't pack our habits and quirks along with the furniture, we lug them with us nonetheless.

Truth is, we take ourselves with us wherever we go. Which also means that we make our own messes, and in time—even years later—we clean them up.

❧

There's a particular rhythm to the van driving down the street, braking, stopping briefly, then moving on. The driver isn't looking for street numbers; he's eyeing other people's castoffs. The days before rubbish pickup are always fruitful for those van-driving hunter-gatherers. In a given week, the curbside offerings might include a toaster oven, a washing machine, mini-blinds, a three-foot palm. The speed at which these items vanish depends on several variables—the weather, competition from neighboring rubbish piles, and the apparent quality of the discards.

When I've tossed out old plants, for instance, their market value can usually be gauged by their longevity on the street. If a plant lasts more than a day, its fate has indeed withered. A better plant, on the other hand, may be gone in under an hour. The local scavengers are no fools—they grab the good stuff and leave the junk.

So it was that my newly deceased television was carted out to the sidewalk the other day, in advance of rubbish pickup. Later, while taking a walk, I happened to see the rival offerings in the area, which seemed more modest than usual. I did, however, notice another television a couple of blocks away—older, smaller, less hunt-worthy than mine.

Even on the "donor" end of the transaction, one wants to put up a sporting effort.

Day One passed without a taker, and Day Two went the same. Day Three was a sleepy Sunday, gray and cool, with little activity outdoors. There were fewer cars than usual, and fewer people out walking. So, the occasional sounds of a front door shutting, or a man calling out to his dog, were more pronounced than usual. The only sound I couldn't identify resembled construction noise—perhaps the hammering of a fence, or some other household repair.

When the sound persisted for a couple of minutes, I peeked out the window. Through the evergreens, I saw two young boys kicking the daylights out of my old television. Then one of them ran over to our driveway and grabbed an enormous rock from the garden. Newly armed, he charged back to the sidewalk and hurled the rock right through the television screen. Then came the sound of exploding glass, followed by the hoots and screams of two self-satisfied little boys, running up the street.

Later when I went outside to survey the damage, I was startled by the ferocity of it. Never mind the glass strewn all over the sidewalk. The television looked like earthquake rubble—strands of loose wire, plastic shards, random parts just hanging. And that huge rock sat embedded in the guts of the machine.

By any standard, what I had witnessed was a form of property crime, victimless and without need for recompense. In fact, the boys had destroyed aspiring rubbish. The television was, after all, waiting at curbside. The larger "crime" was arguably their trespassing through our driveway and stealing that giant rock.

There are countless ways to view this bizarre recreational act committed by two young boys in broad daylight. The one that sticks is that, fortunately, no one and nothing of consequence was actually hurt. Those rookie vandals, maybe eight- and twelve-years-old, in their royal blue T-shirts, give fresh meaning to the term "gratuitous violence."

～⚓～

I had been duly warned. "You won't like Milton," my friend cautioned about the carpenter she was recommending. Milton had tiled a floor in my friend's house and she was glad to be rid of him. He had irked her with his whiny voice and peculiar habits. But he showed up and got the job done, which was, after all, what he was hired to do.

"Liking Milton isn't the point," I countered. "New shingles and downspouts are."

And with that, I hired Milton—middle-aged, paunchy, and bald—to fix assorted odds and ends at our old house. Looking at the list of repairs, Milton estimated that it would take a week, maybe two, at most. He started in October. Unbeknownst to us, his first few days on the job were an early warning signal. It would rain, or dip below freezing, or otherwise prove unsuitable for Milton to work.

It quickly became clear, however, that no weather suited him. Even dry, cool days couldn't guarantee that he'd show up.

Winter slid into a deep freeze, and Milton was temporarily off the hook. Surely we didn't expect him to climb ladders on top of the ice. Still, an entire addition went up on the house next door, while Milton carried on about the cold.

Come spring, Milton phoned to restart the job. But spring was just a date on the calendar, not an honest change of season, and two more months passed with no sign of him. After some prompting on my part, and the threat of hiring someone else, Milton's mood changed. Suddenly he was showing up—two, three days in a row—putting in his version of a long day. He would roll in at the crack of noon, break for lunch at three, return at four, and pack up by five. He had reinvented the workweek.

Whenever I'd look outside to see what Milton was doing, it always surprised me. One day, I heard water running in front of the house—Milton was cleaning the front steps before patching an area with concrete. When I happened to peek outside, he was hosing down a car parked on the street. I assumed that some bits of concrete, or other residue, must have flown that way. I could only imagine the driver returning to the scene of a stranger, unsolicited, washing his car.

But much of the time when I peered outside, I'd see Milton staring at the gutters, or staring at a pillar, or staring into space. Perhaps he was engrossed in some carpenter's reverie, or calculating angles of the next repair. That the job was now actually moving along, and not slowly, became increasingly a source of mystery. Our vanishing contractor, quirks and all, was defying the odds.

Home contractors and their work rank high on lists of consumer complaints. Reliability is not their forte. Yet Milton was totally reliable when it came to calling. He wouldn't hesitate to phone and enumerate the problems with last week's weather, the upcoming forecast, or the excuse du jour that would preclude his showing up. Then, remarkably, the job was done. The virtual carpenter who barely showed up at all had managed to repair every item on our list.

There's no easy way to account for Milton, his unusual work ethic, or his oddly efficient style of carpentry. He came, he sawed, he conquered. And now, thankfully, he's gone.

꿈ﾉ

World War II had ended, housing was cheap, and they were ready to start a family. My parents bought a Tudor, on a half-acre lot, in a suburb of Boston.

When I think of growing up in that house, I picture various images: the chocolate layer cake, shaped like a bungalow, that appeared on my birthday; baseball games in the backyard; holiday dinners. I can picture my childhood bed filled with stuffed animals, and me, scrunched at the mattress's edge.

It's many years since I lived in that house, but I could easily navigate through it blindfolded. That assumes, of course, that the layout remains unchanged.

But in the 1990s, my father sold the house to a young doctor. Relocating from out of state, the doctor had decided that Boston would be his permanent home, a place to settle down and raise a family. Never mind that there was no mate on the horizon, or that he'd just broken up with his fiancée.

The good doctor's tenure, however, proved to be unexpectedly brief. He lasted just long enough to ruin the landscaping and reinvent the best part of the house. As I recall, he planned to tear down the breakfast nook and "open up" the kitchen—that is, to destroy one of the quirky vintage aspects of the house, in favor of a latter-day great room.

Outside he felled a stand of mature evergreens, a source of privacy and shade, leaving the first-floor windows exposed. In their stead, he planted some puny flowers, tiny blotches of color that looked strange and misplaced.

After the doctor left, my phone started to ring.

"Have you seen what's happened to your old house?" a friend gasped.

"Can you believe what they're doing?" shrieked another.

My curiosity had been piqued.

Since I still lived in the area, it was easy enough to drive by—harder not to drive right off the road. Bulldozers, backhoes, and cement trucks lined the driveway and the street. Signs of construction were everywhere.

Was it possible that a new house was sprouting up in our backyard?

It was.

The next owner of our house was reportedly a contractor who decided to put that lot of land to work. He plunked a two-story Colonial on our old baseball diamond and shredded any hope for future privacy. Suddenly greed had gulped up the tranquil view out back. Our yard had become history.

"Why don't you go to the Open House next week?" a friend suggested.

The idea was tempting.

Our old house was up for sale yet again, the search for a third owner in seven years under way. But when I considered the changes that I already knew about, I decided against it. In only seven years, a doctor, then a contractor, had rearranged our family's early life. They did what homeowners naturally do: They imprinted themselves on the house and, in so doing, erased parts of the history that preceded them.

In fact, the house as it now stands is no longer the place where I grew up. The shell may be the same, but the spirit of the place has changed. Going back to one's childhood home always carries that risk, especially if one's memories have been carted off in the renovations.

CHAPTER TWO: HABITS AND ROUTINES

"**N**o dishes in the sink."

That was the rule in my mother's house when I was growing up. The rule wasn't ironclad, but it was clear that the sundry snacks we ate during the day were to be made invisible. We were to leave no remnants in the sink—no dirty dishes for my mother to wash.

The practical basis for the rule was simple: all those glasses and plates piling up were a collision waiting to happen. The logic made sense; it was the psychology that I failed to grasp. My mother claimed that confronting a sink full of dishes first thing in the morning was no way to start the day.

"It makes me want to crawl back into bed," she would say.

To my adolescent way of thinking, her attitude seemed extreme. How could a few soiled plates ruin one's day?

But fast forward a few decades.

It's a generation later and the metaphor has changed: the dishes in my mother's sink are now papers and files sitting on my desk. Forty years later, I now see what's fundamentally wrong with dirty dishes awaiting one first thing in the morning. They're like tarnish on a new day, a reminder, a throwback, as if yesterday never came to a finite end.

It did, only there are these hangers-on.

I've been negotiating of late with the surface of my desk, trying to align the various appendages of work—files, folders, papers—with the mandates of my psyche. The best arrangement, it seemed, was to stack the papers and files I'd been working on, and place them front-and-center on the desk. As an organizing tactic, this seemed most direct. The next morning would start with a clear hierarchy of tasks, defined, controllable.

The reality, however, was different.

I would arrive at my desk each day to see not folders in need of attention, but a mountain that had to be scaled. The pile was too high, left too little room to navigate, and the air was too thin at the top. The effect of all those files, strategically placed, was suffocating.

It was as if I had never left the office the night before–never picked up the dry cleaning or had dinner with friends; never made calls, read the mail, or heard the late news; never engaged in other forms of life. All of it was eradicated by the shrine that was left to yesterday's work.

Pretending to pick up right where one left off the day before has a strange falseness, as if all those hours of other-life hadn't intervened. They had–and good thing, at that. Otherwise, the sense of things being chronically unfinished would erode the natural division between days. Everything would run together, one day into the next–the sink full of dirty dishes that makes one want to crawl back into bed.

These days, I return papers to their files, and folders to their shelves, and I end each day with a tidy, oversimplified desk. There's no mountain to greet me in the morning–not even a bump on the landscape. A simple list guides me to the work at hand, without a daunting pile stacked neatly under my nose.

This is make-believe at the other end of the spectrum. I now close up shop so decisively for the night as to suggest there are no residues left from the day's work. Each day ends cleanly and the next one starts the same. This is, of course, as ludicrous as pretending that one never really left for the night at all. It's the game played differently; the illusion understood.

☙ ❧

Every Sunday morning without fail, it would land on the front stoop. On my way out, I'd grab the paper and leave it inside for my downstairs neighbor, Dave. It surprised me that Dave, forty-ish, an all-digital sort of guy, would subscribe to the hard-copy edition of a newspaper, but apparently he did. Maybe he wanted a reminder of ink, or of actual page turning.

Then I began to notice that if Dave went out first, he'd leave the newspaper for me, as if I were the intended recipient. Only one thing was clear, which was the unspoken protocol we'd both adopted. Whoever went out first would bring the newspaper inside and leave it for the other. Which left both of us wondering who was actually subscribing to the Sunday edition of *The New York Times.*

Finally, it came up in conversation that neither of us had signed up. Maybe our free copy resulted from some promotion. Or perhaps the driver had extra copies on board and ours was an easy stop along the route. Either way, Dave decided to leave the driver a holiday tip, which made us more than just convenient; we had become enriching. It was a win-win.

This de facto arrangement continued for almost four years—to the tune of some $800 in unpaid revenues. It might have gone on indefinitely had there not been a small glitch at the receiving end.

Last spring, Dave and I were both planning trips for the same month, each making arrangements for mail delivery, packages, plant watering. Dave had already left for vacation when the first Sunday rolled around, and the *Times* arrived as usual. I realized that when I left town soon after, the next Sunday's paper would be lying on the front steps in its screaming blue wrapper, evidence that no one was home. It was time to intervene.

I called the newspaper's home delivery line and explained the unusual circumstances. No, we don't have an account number. No, we have no recent or other invoice detailing the specifics of our Sunday delivery. No, I have no idea how, or why, the paper has been showing up free for nearly four years, but could you please make it stop?

The attendant on the other end of the line was clearly stumped and put me on hold. When she returned, she had yet more questions. She double-checked the street number. She asked the names of everyone who currently lived at our address. Then she peeled back another layer of the mystery: Charges for that paper have been billed to a J. Milborn, and the account is up to date.

"J. Milborn?" I exclaimed.

I allowed as how the Milborns used to live here, but they moved almost four years ago. Surely this wasn't possible.

A free paper, she insisted, was even less likely.

With that eureka moment, my curiosity about our Sunday *Times* turned to disbelief. Frankly $800 seems a hefty price to pay for newspapers one never receives. Worse, J. Milborn, who paid that bill every month for nearly four years, is a professor of economics. If this is the kind of fiscal oversight that informs his profession, we're all in deep trouble.

✥

Was there life before Post-it notes?

Probably. But it wasn't nearly so rich with sticky reminders, clinging memos, and glue-backed lists.

The advent of written reminders is nothing new. But somehow our notes seem to vanish when we most need them. They get buried under papers, books, bills and, yes, other notes.

Nothing so augments the usefulness of a note as its mere presence. Showing up is indeed half the battle.

The distinction between a Post-it and any other breed of note is a fine line—edged with adhesive and ready to stick on the surface of one's choice. Once there, it can serve several functions.

Some Post-its are like grunts, one-word exhortations whose meaning is perfectly clear. "Rubbish," the note declares. This is not a criticism or response to some unwanted remark; it's a command. "Soccer" or "Hairdresser" may be less imposing, but they carry the same weight. We don't need the entire text, just a keyword that gets the barrels to curbside, Tommy to the soccer field, and one's hair to the salon.

I would hate to count the number of Post-its that occupy surfaces in my house. Even worse is the amount of redundancy.

As inveterate note-takers know, repetitive notes are a remote form of nagging. They don't whine, or yell, or scold; they just sit doggedly in multiple sites, waiting for the assigned task to be complete. The reward is not simply that the much-announced chore is done; it's that you can chuck the notes and start afresh. Indeed, you may even renew your acquaintance with the surface below before a new note sprouts up. Surely this must be what it's like for men when they shave off their beards: there's a whole other world under there, a sort of naked truth.

No doubt, there are Post-it users who are just garden-variety note-takers. A shopping list, a memo-on-the-run, are their stock-in-trade. But there's often a cartography to Post-it use—a path that leads from one room to the next, a trail of clues about tasks, projects, even intimate details of a user's life. A good sleuth could easily piece together an entire map of one's daily life, based solely upon these notes. Public though they may be—affixed to the back door, kitchen counter, or front hall mirror—they add up to some strange personal math: the whole of one's Post-it life may be greater than the sum of its parts.

As middle age settles in more firmly each year, I realize the benefit of a strong adhesive attached to any reminder. When I was young, a sharp memory was that adhesive. These days, Post-it notes are a close second.

❧

Global economics is not my forte, nor will I ever be asked to advise on the future of the yen. I can, however, address a more local matter pertaining to the dollar. The common notion is that a dollar is worth, or can be converted to, a hundred cents.

I'm here with proof to the contrary.

I don't know when this started happening, or when I began to notice it. But for years now, I've been undercharged for all manner of goods and services.

In restaurants, the check will arrive at the end of a meal, and I'll see that dessert isn't listed. Or I'll be filling up my car at the service station, and the attendant will ask for $30. He'll have forgotten to charge for the oil. Or recently I was stocking up on household supplies. The cashier handed me the sales slip, which looked suspiciously slight. She had mistakenly omitted the first "1" from a $119 item.

I don't know how often this happens, but it's frequent enough that I'm no longer surprised. Between forgetfulness, bad math, and assorted other blunders, I get considerable bang for my buck.

In fact, however, I don't.

Whenever these incidents occur, I point them out and adjust the bill. Invariably, this triggers one of two remarks: the salesperson, cashier, or waiter thanks me beyond all reason, as if common decency were a form of heroism.

Of course, it's not—but then, it's apparently not so common, either.

Otherwise, the salesperson adopts a belligerent air, as if to ready him- or herself for battle. Questioning a bill, it seems, is often a hostile exchange, where the customer feels ripped-off. As a result, some of these encounters require a couple of go-rounds to clarify that, yes, I am indeed trying to pay more—that is, to pay the appropriate amount. Sometimes battle-weary salespeople will look at me, as if to say, "Lady, you got to be kidding!"

But consider the math: I'm just one individual who's in the habit of checking the tab and counting the change. Multiply my situation times a few million consumers, and the numbers start to add up. If I'm often undercharged, surely this must be happening to countless others, and often without their knowledge.

In the end, if this is a trend, then someone is paying for all that cash that goes uncollected. It's safe to assume that you and I are the ones who pay in the form of higher prices for desserts, engine oil, and household goods.

This isn't a case of global economics so much as it is basic math. If undercharging is a common malady in the business world, the impact is obvious. An undercharge is an accidental gain for someone—and a loss for all of us.

✌ ✌

In a more perfect world, certain chores would complete themselves. Laundry, for instance, would require only that we shuttle the contents from one machine to the next. Smart clothes, as they might be called, would "know" to fold themselves and return to their designated shelves.

Of course, in a really perfect world, smart clothes would also be self-cleaning; they would eliminate the need for laundry altogether. Spin cycles would refer only to the laundering of news items, not to washing machines past.

The world is, alas, not that perfect.

As with so many things, there's more to laundry than meets the eye. At first glance, laundry appears to be about the act of cleaning. In fact, however, clean isn't the goal, but a mere stage in the process. The real goal is invisibility—clothes that are clean, folded, and stored away.

There are those who take pleasure in the simple catharsis of laundry—the fact that what was dirty only hours before is now clean. Some people are also calmed by the act of repetitive folding. And there are those who enjoy the rhythmic certainty of load after load being transferred from washer to dryer to basket to drawer.

Yet there are those who get stuck on the arithmetic of it all. How quickly an article of dirty clothing adds up to one pile, then multiple piles, and then it's laundry time all over again. Laundry is never individual pieces, itemized. It's collective. It multiplies.

And there's another phase that defies all the orderly increments that partisans seem to enjoy. A pile of clean clothes, unsorted, unfolded, is nearly as bothersome as the same pile before it's washed. Sure, the clothes are clean. But the task is still nowhere near complete.

Isn't laundry, at bottom, about trading dirty for clean? About the consummate act of recycling?

In part, yes. But it's also about starting over, wherein we pluck clean shirts and socks from a drawer, closet, or shelf.

This is the beginning and end of all laundry: not the cleaning itself, but the orchestration of items into rows, stacks, and groups—ready, waiting, invisible. Without these orchestrated effects, clean clothes would have the same rumpled disarray as their dirty counterparts.

Reality is just the half of it. The perception of clean, with its neatly turned folds and edges, tucked away, may well be the better half.

❦

It was the end of the meal and time to consider dessert. My friend asked for a cup of coffee, I ordered carrot cake. When the waitress disappeared from view, my friend leaned over and asked, "Are you feeling all right?"

I had apparently crossed some invisible line, breached some fixed insight that my friend held about me. I had failed to order one of the chocolate items on the list. My friend had never witnessed such a detour, felt sure that it signified something. And it did: my growing realization that not all desserts have to be chocolate; that not all chocolate satisfies; and that much of what passes for chocolate is hardly worthy of the name. I had come to this revelation rather late in the game, a few too many Dove Bars after the fact.

There are those who might consider this view traitorous in someone who claims to love chocolate. To me, it merely reflects the evolution of my sweet tooth, if such a thing can be said to evolve.

In my newly liberated state, I now choose desserts filled with all manner of fruits. Not that I ever disliked them; sacrificing chocolate on their behalf just seemed a dubious trade. But I have seen the light, flaky crust of other pastries and taken heed.

Chocolate is the least of the changes I've undergone in recent years. Blue, which was once my favorite color, remains so, if less exclusively. I now eye other colors with a more open mind, aware of their possibilities. So, too, my views on education, television, driving, and a host of other issues. As the culture has changed, some of my views have changed in response. The single, all-purpose answer—the chocolate-only dessert—now seems simplistic and confining.

Nor is the range of personal change that we accept in others all that limited. There are those who leave safe, established careers in favor of some untested yearning. We admire their pluckiness. One-time Democrats cross party lines to become Republicans—think Ronald Reagan. And according to a Gallup survey, some 40 percent of Americans describe themselves as "born again."

Could there be a more fundamental change?

Generally, we regard these shifts as a product of age and experience, a recognition that we outgrow certain positions and adopt others. If that weren't the case, we'd all be stuck in some hapless adolescence, wanting the keys to the car.

As an election year approaches, we would do well to recall the breadth of change that we allow our friends, family, and colleagues. Changes of heart or mind are often just that—natural shifts that take place gradually, over many years. When our friends or family announce that they no longer feel a certain way, or hold a certain belief, we don't see them as "slippery" or "flip-flopping," terms we reserve for politicians. We acknowledge the changed stance and try to glean the process by which it occurred.

Even public officials, for all their flavor-of-the-day politics, can undergo real and legitimate change.

CHAPTER THREE: FOOD

L ast night a friend came over for dinner. Since the occasion of my cooking is about as common as a lunar eclipse, my friend was curious.

"So, are you more like Rachel or Julia?" she inquired.

"Neither," I laughed.

Truth is, I started cooking again last winter after a hiatus of nearly twenty years. Of course, I ate during that time. Good local take-out and numerous restaurants conspired to keep me happily out of the kitchen.

Then this unforeseen reversal. It started with a hunch and a few grievances. Several of my favorite restaurant dishes—Szechuan green beans, for one—seemed needlessly lacquered up, oiled beyond reason. Surely their virtues would brighten without all that oil.

Or I'd be eating a frozen chicken-and-pasta dinner, impressed with the flavoring, but annoyed by the skimpy portion. The list of ingredients looked suspiciously long and unpronounceable, aimed largely, it seemed, at preserving what little was there.

These and other episodes drove me back to the kitchen. Call it a case of late-onset cooking, for it came on suddenly, without warning, and shows no signs of letting up.

Unlike Rachel and Julia, who arrive with their arsenals of books, recipes, and knowledge, I come to the kitchen with a modest résumé. My weapons of choice are a few good instincts and a willingness to fail.

In the matter of failing, let me be frank. For my purposes, cookbooks offer ideas and possibilities, not formulas that I'm meant to follow. Besides, many recipes tend to be too ornate, calling for more fuss than is needed. If four ingredients can do the work of ten, I'll gladly scrap the remaining six. Which is to say that my cooking style, if it may be called that, combines equal parts guesswork, science project, and luck.

It was a bad guess and a luckless day when I took on fresh crabmeat. Whatever I originally had in mind escapes me now as I recall that night. I sautéed the crabmeat and watched the color go from light cream to tan to murky beige. As the texture turned limp, so, too, did my interest. No doubt, a real cook would have countered with a triage plan—some brilliant herbs, chunks of mango, something wholly unexpected. But the scruffy beigeness of the entire enterprise stopped me cold. I decided to cut my losses and let it go. The best that could be said of the crabmeat is that it was edible—sort of.

Other experiments have proved more fruitful. One day I sliced a pear into eight or so disks and pan-fried them in a sesame-ginger marinade. Somehow sliced pear, lightly charred with sesame, takes on the flavor of maple syrup. For those of us with a sweet tooth, this is heavenly.

Somewhere between these extremes, I've found my stride in the kitchen. I've liberated Szechuan green beans from so much oil and embellished the chicken-and-pasta, in both flavor and portion. My culinary improvisations have led to surprises that are worth repeating and others that bear retelling for their sheer folly. Perhaps if I paid more attention to Rachel or Julia, my cooking would be more reliable. As it stands, I enjoy the occasional side of suspense along with my meals.

꧁꧂

If you've watched cooking competitions on television, you know the standards by which they're judged—originality, presentation, and taste are the typical trio. Among them, presentation may be the trickiest of the lot. Even the natural hotties of the food world— think plums and tomatoes—can lack flavor, while some of the best burgers and cottage cheese fall short in the looks department. Frumpiness in a food has little to do with taste. So it comes to the business of "plating," as they call it, to gussy up the wallflowers.

A simple dish, arrayed with a drizzle of this, a dash of that, can become a visual feast. The art of plating is no less than the choreography of elements balanced for overall effect. Add bits of architecture and geometry (lengths of pasta, wedges of melon), whimsy and color (sprigs, sprinkles, dots), and even the plainest foods gain dimension and depth. Plating can be a form of alchemy, adding visual spice in places where there was none.

It stands to reason that certain foods need more primping than others—the oatmeals of the world, for instance, are at an obvious disadvantage. Surely oatmeal is better suited to staving off hunger than accenting a bowl. Logic would dictate, then, that serving a larger portion adds nothing by way of aesthetics.

Which brings us to the matter of potatoes. The old-fashioned Russet, simply baked, is a stalwart at the American table. We forgive its lumpish appearance because of the flavor and comfort it imparts. A perfectly baked Russet, its skin nearing parchment, with a dollop of sour cream is a full-bodied, satisfying food. Just don't look too closely, as conventional beauty—or beauty of any kind, really—is not its forte.

On numerous occasions in recent months, I've ordered a baked potato in restaurants. To describe these potatoes as "large" fails to do them justice. Last week, when a waitress delivered my dinner, I couldn't resist asking whether the potato had been on steroids. It didn't just dominate the plate; it dwarfed a grilled chicken sandwich that was duly plump in its own right. Indeed, that sandwich played second fiddle to a sprawling, bloated spud that, at seven inches and three-quarters of a pound, looked more like a rat. Only the tail and snout were missing.

Frankly, no amount of "plating" could have dressed up, or toned down, the grotesque geometry of this meal. Only a more sensible potato could have done that.

I've eaten at other, often fancier, restaurants, where the potatoes also took on lives of their own. It's hard to know whether this is management's idea of good value, or a case of agriculture gone awry. I will note for the record, however, that I saw a rat darting across the street as I drove home from the restaurant last week. I could swear it was smaller than the potato on my plate.

✌ॐ✌

First, a confession: I no longer allow peanut butter in my home. Why? Because my delivery system of choice isn't a conventional knife, but a spoon. Spoon to jar to mouth, direct transit, no stops along the way.

Yet variations on this product are perfectly safe in my house. Thai peanut sauce, peanut butter cookies, peanut brittle—delicious all, but without the pure temptation that is peanut butter.

Of course, it's easy to dismiss a childhood staple for its sticky, lowbrow simplicity. For its assertiveness and inability to play well with others, its preference for the virtuoso role. Most sauces that originate with peanut butter are bullies, trouncing other ingredients. Chicken with peanut sauce, for instance, too often tastes like, well, peanut sauce.

Or consider the beloved Reese's Peanut Butter Cup, with its attempt at power-sharing. Though the chocolate shell makes itself known, the product name all but declares the winner.

Like few other foods, peanut butter can embody one's childhood in a few essential images: blue metal lunchbox, green canoe, redwood picnic table. In these scenarios, the peanut butter of my 1960s youth was always paired with strawberry jam, and sandwiched between slices of Wonder Bread, reassuringly soft and white. At that stage in our nation's dietary evolution, there was little talk of rustic, locally sourced whole grains. Breads were divided by function—subs, dinner rolls, pizza crust. Even pita pockets had yet to go mainstream.

But as our nutritional vistas expanded, so, too, did our vocabulary. We now live in a world of low-fat, farm-raised, free-range foods. With all of that hyphenation came greater awareness of the conditions (and politics) that affect what we eat.

So where does that leave old-fashioned peanut butter?

Too often, people regard it as a throwback, a childish relic, an emergency food with good protein and shelf life, suitable for a blizzard or extended power outage. In other words, it's a food with purpose, even if eating it isn't high on the list.

But peanut butter is so much more: it's the ultimate blend of salty and sweet, better than candy, the perfect solo act. In combination with jam, it's better still.

If you haven't eaten a PB&J sandwich in recent memory, do yourself a favor. As you've surely seen in the grocery aisle, peanut butter now comes in a dozen self-righteous variations, some more flavorful than others. So, slather a non-GMO, organic version on the artisanal bread of your choice.

Or go retro, as I do, and revert to the Skippy or Jif of your youth. Close your eyes and take a bite. The reward is twofold: a rich, complex grownup treat that's far better than you recall, along with a vintage piece of your past.

❧❦

Breakfast has long been billed as the most important meal of the day. I couldn't agree more since, without it, many perfectly civil people become less so. As one of them, I should know. My breakfast routine was recently upended, forcing me to reconsider the whole enterprise.

For years now, my breakfast has consisted of cottage cheese on crackers, with tea to drink. Simple enough, one would think. But I've come to realize that what passed for simplicity was a series of habits and assumptions that were hardly simple at all.

Consider, first, the architectural component. It's a full eight-ounce cup of cottage cheese that I spoon onto three crackers—a true test of the crackers' sturdiness and load tolerance. Since cottage cheese tends to disregard boundaries, I carefully bank the sides of the crackers. I'm aiming for a mound effect with little or no spillage. Nor are the crackers just a platform for cottage cheese; they add both flavor and texture to the meal. If that's a lot of engineering first thing in the day, then so be it.

Every now and then, however, reality impinges and substitutions are needed. In this case, the full-bodied soda crackers that I'd used for years suddenly vanished from the supermarket. No product tag remained, no hint of the item that had long occupied the shelf. Instead some lesser biscuits promptly filled in the space, as if my crackers had never existed.

Puzzled by this turn of events, I drove to four different supermarkets. No luck. For whatever reason, my trusted crackers were apparently being phased out and so, too, I feared, my longstanding breakfast.

I tried various alternatives. First was a biscuit whose richness overwhelmed the cottage cheese. The next one was too sweet. The third had, well, design issues.

It never occurred to me that my breakfast had, among its prerequisites, a critical configuration: My old crackers were square with rounded corners. Those corners provided something to grab on to. Without them, I admit, more than a few cheese-laden crackers slipped through my fingers, never making it to my mouth. My foray into the realm of round crackers was a complete bust.

Who knew that geometry could be a salient feature of breakfast?

Continuing my search, I stumbled upon an old favorite of my father's, a long rectilinear chowder cracker with the requisite corners and the right balance of flavors. It also had a structural advantage: it was a workhorse, able to carry a daunting load of cottage cheese with neither spills nor breakage. Such impressive stats made me an instant convert.

Eventually I did, in fact, find a source for my old square biscuits, but it no longer mattered. Survival of the fittest, it turns out, applies even to crackers.

I stopped by a local bakery recently in search of a snack. As I surveyed the options, I got to thinking about stocking up on snacks for my freezer. When the clerk turned my way, I pointed to the showcase and asked if a particular pastry could be frozen. She stared at me blankly, uncomprehending.

"Can these be frozen?" I asked again.

Still no response. So I changed tactics, trying a different form of the word.

"Can I freeze these crullers?"

Her eyebrows lifted.

"Free?" she said, with a foreign accent. "Free? No, they're seventy-five cents each."

I gave her the money, and left with a cruller, amused and exasperated. I bought nothing for the freezer. Though I'd solved the problem at hand, I failed to make even the slightest dent in the larger issue—that, in much of my daily life, my American-born English seems more like a foreign tongue.

It wasn't always that way.

When I was growing up in the '50s and '60s, everyone, it seemed, spoke English. Sure, there were accents from different parts of the world, but people made themselves understood, natives and foreigners alike. It never occurred to me, as an American kid growing up in her homeland, that I spoke the dominant tongue. I spoke what everyone spoke—or so I thought.

Now, as an adult, I'm keenly aware that my fluent, well-manicured English seems almost quaint—just one more tool that gets me no closer to the pastries I want.

The fact is, many American cities are beyond simply diverse. Not long ago, I received a mailing from a state agency. At the bottom, listed in more than a dozen languages, was the suggestion that non-English speakers have the mailing translated.

Whatever one's origins, the fact remains that for many of us, there are basically two kinds of people: those who speak your language and those who don't. At the least, a tension naturally exists where a common language doesn't.

Consider this scenario. A friend and I have been getting lunch at a certain Thai restaurant for several years. Sometimes we eat there, sometimes we order to go. Over time, the particulars of our order have become well-known to the staff. Then the restaurant changed hands and we had to begin from scratch.

Our first encounters with the new crew were fairly simple. The hostess gave us a menu, we pointed to the items we wanted, we signaled how we'd like the dishes flavored—two stars of spiciness, not just one.

Placing the same order by phone, however, was another story. With no menu at the ready, and nothing to point to, we would hang by the thread of whatever words we had in common. Sometimes, alas, those words were too few, and another voice would come on the line to rescue our order.

But as the weeks went by, a certain rapport was developing. At the restaurant, the new hostess and I would smile at each other, glad to be able to exchange pleasantries. Over the phone, she now recognized my voice, the details of my order, the familiar name. Then one day on the phone, we ran into a glitch.

In a previous conversation, I thought we had resolved the issue of spiciness by designating "two stars." So I tried that again—twice. When she clearly didn't understand, I tried the words "hot," then "spicy." The air got tangled in frustration. Next thing I knew, a male coworker, more fluent in English, was summoned to the phone to puzzle through the order.

I got off the phone feeling like the ugly American, fast-talking and hungry, too rushed to speak slowly enough for this gracious foreigner.

"It made me sad," the hostess said of our botched phone call when I arrived for my takeout.

I nodded apologetically. I shrugged my shoulders and made

a self-mocking Pac-Man gesture with my hand, as if to say that we all speak too fast in our own language. When I deliberately slowed down for emphasis, she laughed at the strange, strained sound of English in slow motion.

There was no winning, perhaps, but at least we had arrived at a compromise. If there was a struggle, it wasn't mine or hers, one or the other, with blame attached. There was plainly a gap between us, oceans and continents that needed a bridge.

While language is always a fine tool, patience should be the common tongue.

❧❦❧

Whenever I go out to dinner, I start with the same thing: Diet Coke, no ice. Most of the time, the server gets it right. But not infrequently, my drink will arrive with ice, thereby doubling the server's task. Of course, the drink can be removed and a new one brought in its place. But what of the diner's confidence in the up-coming meal? If "no ice" is too taxing, what lies ahead? I mention this since most servers jot such details on a pad, so there's no heavy lifting in the memory department. If they look at their notes, it's all there.

Fast forward to the other night when four of us ate dinner at a little Italian place. The menu listed both standards and specials, all with their own accompaniments. As it happened, each of us placed an order that veered slightly off-course. There was the swap of eggplant for snap peas, of sweet potatoes for rice. Would it be possible to get a center cut of salmon? Though the list of quirks and variations was long, our waitress—fortyish, wiry, efficient—was unfazed. She took it all in, glad to accommodate.

Nor did she write down a single word.

Unarmed with paper or pen, she listened to each order with its sundry detours, then she'd nod. No repeating after we spoke to clarify or confirm. There was just that nod, an occasional question, an air of competence. All the while, she was making small talk.

I couldn't wait to see the outcome of this little magic trick. With all the fine points that go into a meal—presentation, timing, service—memorization barely makes it onto the list.

After all, why should it matter if a waitress knows by heart the details of every diner's meal? Isn't that just a sideshow that can divert from the main event? And isn't that the very point of writing it down?

Frankly, if magic were to be part of the program, I'd prefer a juggling act, maybe a card trick, over this culinary sleight of hand. No doubt the spectacle of such mental gymnastics can be impressive. It can add considerably to the meal—especially by way of errors. (I keep thinking of those misplaced ice cubes in so many Diet Cokes.)

Besides, in most aspects of life, we're told to make copies, backups, contingencies. The lack of even the most basic notes—just some hieroglyphs—is asking for trouble.

Maybe if I knew the waitress's technique—was she using some mnemonic device or thinking, "Sweater, beard, flank steak rare"?—I'd be more amenable to the idea. But I couldn't help envisioning a head full of conflicting orders, a cacophony of tables, diners, and details that had written-off a time-honored tradition.

Oh, for a few slips of paper.

In the end, dinner went without a hitch. Our waitress brought each plate to the proper person, its particulars exactly as requested. Personally, if I owned a restaurant, I'd want a wait staff of scribes, not illusionists. Panache is nice; accuracy is better. Our waitress, thankfully, delivered on both.

☙❧

You find a breakfast cereal that you love, the perfect jeans, a tennis racquet whose grip fits yours just so. These things don't change your life, but they register in the brain, activating some tiny pleasure sensor.

In your own microsphere, that momentary crunch of cereal just before the milk engulfs it contains a meeting of matter and mind. All is not well with the world, by any stretch; but for a few seconds there, and in the quirkiest way, you've found the ultimate fit. Call it the Match.com of product placement, minus the questionnaire and the awkward dates.

So it goes that once you've used a product for years, and can't imagine life without it, it vanishes.

When I find a product that I really like, I don't just buy it. I preempt the inevitable runs on inventory by amassing my own. No, I don't secretly think the whole world wants what I want (though one can never be too sure). Nor do I tend to hoard.

But it takes only a few like-minded sorts to permanently strip a product from the shelves. So I share new product finds gingerly—preferably with those who live out-of-town and won't strain the local supply.

The exact opposite holds true when it comes to dining out. When I like a restaurant, I share that fact with as wide a range of people as possible. Unlike consumers who stock up on goods, zealous diners have few options to ensure that their favorite eateries will survive.

I know this firsthand.

Years back, I found the best Chinese food I'd ever tasted. The restaurant was nearby, the owner an elegant Chinese man determined to prepare his native cuisine without compromise. No sooner did I learn his name (George), and he learn my standing order (Szechuan green beans, slightly burnt) than the restaurant closed.

A succession of restaurants followed—seafood, Korean, and Japanese, to name a few. At some point, new owners didn't even make the pretense of renovating; they'd slap a new sign on the door, and that was that.

For a while, I considered myself a restaurant jinx. If I really fell for a place, it was doomed. But then I reconsidered: restaurants fail, regardless of my affections. I may miss George and those green beans, but he had apparently set up shop in the wrong place. The list of failed restaurants that followed was clear evidence.

If there's a lesson here, it's that our loyalties in the material world have only limited traction. Products come and go, as do restaurants, and our devotion is worth only so much. Finding a new tennis racquet, cereal, or pair of jeans isn't the issue.

Of course we find replacements; they're just not the same. With love, it never is.

CHAPTER FOUR: AT WORK

It has been sitting on a chair for the last four days while I waver back and forth. Should I throw out the dictionary that I've used for twenty-five years, that has all but fallen apart? Or should I grant yet another stay of execution, and return it to its shelf?

The issue should be simple, the answer obvious. But then there's the matter of history.

I don't recall when this particular dictionary became a fixture in my life; it's just the one, among several, that I automatically turn to. It graduated with me from dorm to apartment to house, so that I no longer remember being without it.

As in any long-standing relationship, the rules, over time, have changed. There have been periods when I've depended on the dictionary for its articulated view of the world. Other times, I've had doubts and checked rival sources to confirm a particular meaning. On balance, the dictionary has served me ably and well. In turn, I have provided support: I have glued, taped, and otherwise struggled with a binding that has resisted even my best therapeutic efforts. For years now, the covers and spine have been a patchwork of fixes—black tape here, beige there, and none of it terribly effective.

So this is what's left: the dictionary no longer qualifies as a single book; it has become a three-volume set—fully bound, partially bound, and unabashedly loose-leaf. It is this latter section, in the center, with its hundred or so uncommitted pages, that has become a problem. Somewhere between "jettison" and "lunatic," all hell broke loose, and the words came unhinged from their proper home.

In theory, this whole issue was put to rest several years ago. A friend, appalled by the state of my ancient dictionary, gave me the perfect gift—a new edition. In practice, however, it sat idle on a shelf. I would use it on occasion, aware of its rigid covers and the general stiffness of its demeanor. More often, though, I would dig out the old volume to search out the word in question. It hardly seemed to matter that, little by little, the old dictionary was decomposing in my hands. Given the physical facts of the situation, it's hard to defend the long afterlife I've conferred upon this book.

What is it that I fear?

It's the loss of that trusted counsel that could define a concept, settle an argument, even win a bet. It was the final authority when authority was needed. Moreover, anyone whose work revolves around language knows the value of a good dictionary. It's a writer's equivalent of old blue jeans, reliable and reassuring.

So there are reasons for the dictionary's tenure on my shelf and for its current holding pattern on the chair. But enough. Today it will become part of the assembled rubbish that waits at curbside to leave for good. Lately I admit to looking at the "new" dictionary with an eye toward the future. It's sturdy and solid and current in a way that the old one ceased to be.

Still, despite all reason and common sense, part of me feels like a traitor.

❧❧

Retractions are the bane of every newspaper's existence. Getting it wrong—whether it's the slant of a story, or specific facts—is bad on all fronts. In the world of news, such errors can reflect badly on the subject, the journalist, and the publication itself. Since credibility is a newspaper's chief asset, the consequences couldn't be greater. Even benign errors, when they appear often enough, undermine the fabric of a publication. Still there are other reasons that stories get derailed, which can also compromise the truth.

Consider this scenario. Twenty-plus years ago, as a young journalist, I was assigned an article by a respected magazine. The piece was to be a full-length feature, with numerous interviews, about a medical clinic. I researched the facility, interviewed its director and several former patients, spoke with other specialists in the field, and gathered background.

When I submitted the piece to the magazine, my editor wanted more. She asked me to "punch it up," as I recall, to give it more spice. I went back to the drawing board and checked my notes. I made some changes, tweaking this detail, embellishing that, all within the bounds of what I knew to be true.

When I handed in the revised copy, the editor still wasn't satisfied. She wanted to know why my article contained no superlatives—no references to groundbreaking research, or leading authorities, or top-ranking position. My response didn't please her: the clinic was neither groundbreaking, nor leading in its authority, and it wasn't top-ranked. Truth is, it was the only facility of its kind in the region, practicing techniques pioneered by others, and quietly known for its good work.

In the course of talking with the editor, I realized that my article wasn't the problem—reality was. My editor was hoping for a blockbuster story about the renowned institute she imagined the clinic to be. Instead I had written a truthful account of the workaday place that the clinic actually was. We had reached a standoff, and the article never ran.

That episode reveals not only a problem of expectation and pressure, but something fundamental about language. Superlatives sell: the biggest, best, first, and most will always win attention. It's everything else that needs proper shading and nuance.

Writing about extremes is the easy part; it's the other 99 percent of life—the vast grayscale of ordinary experience—that gets interesting. Hyperbole is tempting for its drama; no doubt, the best storytellers are dramatists at heart. Yet the bulk of daily life falls into that midrange lacking the polarity of black and white, to say nothing of intense color.

Some journalists assess their goals in terms of achieving a certain rank within a news organization, writing books, perhaps winning awards. A more internal goal, however, might be to portray increasingly complex ideas with vividness and clarity. Writing colorfully about shades of gray will always pose a challenge.

꙳꙳

It's daunting, that blank surface, staring back at me. It is demanding and austere, makes me feel as if I have to perform.

"Something you don't like?" it seems to suggest. "Well, learn to live with it."

And so, I do.

What I'm learning to live with is, well, paper—a dozen pads of the white lined variety, in standard legal size, with a bound strip at the top. That narrow strip, with its swirled dark brown, is all that keeps me from hating these pads. It is the one salvation from all this whiteness.

I have no objection to white in theory, principle, or bridal wear. It's just that lined paper, for this writer, cannot be white. This is no different, really, from insisting upon a certain amount of cream in one's coffee, the right amount of toothpaste on the brush, or the car visor tilted at a certain angle. These are small, everyday things about which we tend to be particular—persnickety, even.

So, too, in our working lives. An accountant may prefer to use a certain calculator, a carpenter his own drill. The tools of one's trade are hardly generic; over time, they become part of one's signature.

The surface on which I prefer to write is a yellow lined pad, softer than white, more pleasing to my eye. When I look at its empty lines, it doesn't stare back—it simply waits. And in its way, it invites my participation. It encourages without making demands. The simple fact is that yellow, with its mild pallor, lacks the punch and luster of white. To me, its deficiency is a prime asset: it doesn't impose the stark contrast of dark ink on white tablet—it has no such attitude.

White paper, on the other hand, seems loud and annoying. As I write in longhand, crossing out words here and there, I see my foibles in a different light. The line that deletes a certain phrase is no longer a thought unfolding as I go. On a white page, the cross-out becomes an announcement: "Thought aborted; new thought emerging." It jolts and jars. It's like the three-way mirror in a dressing room: Who needs to see all those bulges and wrinkles when a single reflection would do?

That's why we have tailors—and second drafts.

An architect I know confirms the primacy of this issue in the matter of tracing paper. "Trace," as she calls it, comes in several colors and textures, each with its own properties. In her view, white is always the preference; yellow is the color one tolerates.

One can look at these distinctions and wonder at the sheer prissiness of those who make them. Or one can recognize that we all have our own versions of yellow and white, whether at the dinner table, the office, or in the car.

I have seven white pads left from the original dozen. They will be a continuing source of annoyance for as long as my yellow pads are out of stock. Of course, some would argue that I should simply forego paper, that dinosaur of writing surfaces, in favor of the computer. Then the entire process of thinking, crossing-out, revising would become a seamless lie, as if the mind could skate from start to finish without tripping or stumbling along the way. First, second, third drafts—they would be indistinguishable one from the next. Blocks of text would simply be moved or deleted without memory of the various stages. There would be no evidence of the process, no messy pages to demonstrate the movement of one's thoughts.

If that's the alternative, give me white lined paper any day.

❧❧❧

We had spoken by phone a few times, and several emails went back and forth. Ed seemed friendly, smart, and thoroughly professional. Then came a business note, written by hand. It was memorable not for its content, but for its unexpected form—words erratically spaced, letters slanting one way, then another, capitals far outsizing their smaller counterparts. "Boston," for instance, was divided in half—first syllable to the left, second to the right—as if the city were at war with itself. And all of it was climbing uphill.

I'm no handwriting expert, but I know odd writing when I see it. This was a kind of script that one would at least wonder, if not worry, about. I suppose one could argue that Ed's was a "creative" hand, unfettered by direction or evenness, or the usual constraints that guide most handwriting. But the tension embedded in his lettering was obvious. This highly professional man looked like a wayward child in print; there was nothing but trouble in that scrawl.

Granted, my dealings with Ed were all business. For all I knew, he could have been a serial killer on the side. This same man also ran a major department at a publishing firm. Clearly he'd achieved more than just creeping people out with his weird handwriting.

Which raises the larger issue of penmanship. Some of the most surprising people have dubious handwriting. Among them are those who are otherwise neat, dapper, or well-coiffed, methodical or deliberate, and those with a flair for the visual. Such folks, one might think, would pen their words in a style similar to their general demeanor. Not necessarily so.

The logic that handwriting should reflect the writer seems, at best, half true. One of the most well-organized, groomed, and visually oriented people I know has unspeakable writing, literally.

Often when she writes a note, I'll have no idea what it says. There are always a few words I can't make out. When I've mentioned this to her, she brushes it off, as if I were scolding her for putting elbows on a dining table.

Penmanship, and one's attitude about it, often reverts to those early lessons where habits and manners mix. Sure, good handwriting is a plus, but not because it's morally better, or more refined, or displays superior manners. It's good because it's easy to read, which is, after all, the point.

If you're trying to communicate, it helps to consider the reader. Otherwise you might as well speak different languages. As it turns out, my well-organized friend has heard countless complaints about her writing. She's had to train an entire office to decode her rushed hand. This may be one of the more subtle perks of being the boss: people will show unusual patience and courtesy trying to figure out what you mean. But given the issue of inscrutable handwriting, it seems arrogant to foist the problem onto prospective readers. It would be like deliberately mumbling, then expecting the listener to know what was said.

Penmanship may be the last vestige of schoolmarmishness. It evokes images of blackboards and notebooks filled with perfectly looped Ls and Bs. But now, in an age of texts and emails, handwriting is, for many, the medium of last resort. Still, it's nice to understand a note the first time around, without second-guessing any of its parts.

✌🏵✍

If you ask a middle-aged person his or her age, there's often a moment of hesitation. It's not that we're coy, or trying to invent a number that's more to our liking; it's an attempt to be specific when vague will usually suffice. If you're in your fifties, for instance, and you've been there for a while, you tend to lose track of age—at least your own. Besides, time is shaped more by the events in one's life than the candles on a cake.

Many of us play a game in which we try to guess the age of others—people in the news, authors, politicians. Then we check the listing or news clip, only to find that we're off, whether up or down, by a decade or more. In this game, winning isn't the point; confirming one's cluelessness is the entire goal. Victory is the shoulder shrug that acknowledges, yes, I truly have no idea how old anyone is.

This is a great equalizer: the realization that age is fickle and deceptive—part genes, part luck, and capable of being altered or rearranged.

Still, two of the more reliable signs of age are books and fillings.

53

If you're over a certain age, chances are you've got lots of each—a home packed with volumes of various sizes and shapes, and teeth filled with silver or gold. Though I won't argue the virtues of fillings over fluoride, I would defend the value of books any day.

In my middle-aged office, bookcases stretch from floor to ceiling, lining an entire wall. Hundreds of books populate certain shelves, while folders fill the rest. I didn't fully grasp the rivalry between these groups until a recent crisis. Many of the books are old favorites, rich with associations and history. The folders, by contrast, are more like weeds—paper begetting more paper. While the folders beg for more space, the books are, frankly, squatters that stay by virtue of having been there for years. History is what earns their place on the shelf.

Perhaps if I were younger, or viewed this as an opportunity to renovate, I'd pack up the books and allow the folders to multiply. But I'm not, and I don't. Those books, some with notations dating back to my college years, form a personal archive of sorts—a layer of self, superimposed on the work of others. Then, too, certain books evoke a particular mood, or memory, or sense of place. To oust these volumes would be to shelve a part of myself on grounds of mere utility.

Perhaps a younger person would do exactly that, and free up some much-needed space. I, on the other hand, will keep the books until I tire of them. That is, after all, one of the perks of age.

CHAPTER FIVE: HEALTH

It looked like countless other bills that arrive in the mail. It was computer-generated, printed on a standard form. The bill was for a routine medical checkup, listing the various services that were performed—comprehensive exam, EKG, blood tests. There was an accounting of which items the insurance company had covered and the balance I owed. In the lower portion of the statement, an area was set aside for "Important Messages Regarding Your Account." In dot-matrix print, it said, "Enjoy May flowers."

Enjoy May flowers?

Suddenly my doctor's bill had become a bumper sticker—an invoice with a bit of common tripe.

In the past, the "messages" section of the bill was reserved for insurance notes or matters related to the services at hand. Frankly, I would have preferred that. The person who oversees one's medical care shouldn't be sending verbal smiley-faces on his bill. It's gooey and unprofessional. In fact, my doctor is a shy, serious man in his sixties, who teaches at Harvard; he's not some Hallmark card with a medical degree.

Why, then, this jarring, commonplace note?

It may be for the same reason that certain car dealers have taken to sending birthday cards to customers. Not long ago, I received one. It's not simply a marketing ploy, or a way of planting themselves in our minds; it's a popular notion about what's user-friendly these days. It juxtaposes different parts of our lives in a way that deliberately surprises. The car dealer doesn't just care about the sale; he cares about me. My doctor isn't concerned solely with my physical health; he cares about my whole being.

Perhaps this is the New Empathy: "I feel your pain" has been replaced by a wish to promote my pleasure.

But "Enjoy May flowers" is really just a variant of "Have a nice day." It's a phrase with more courtesy than content, that has its place in certain kinds of exchanges. It's a space-filler, a sort of punctuation, like "Take care," and other conversation-closers. (Actually, "Take care" would be a more fitting message on a physician's statement.) It's harmless enough, to be sure; it's the banality of it that grates. Besides, if there weren't a culture-wide fear of pauses and empty spaces, there would be no need for these tepid sayings. Conversations would end with simple goodbyes and space allotted for messages on bills would be left blank.

The only mail I want to receive from my car dealer is an occasional reminder that I'm due for a tune-up. For that matter, my doctor could send the same note. That would be useful, appropriate, and welcome. This other business of slogans on bills, disingenuous birthday greetings, and the like, is not as user-friendly as some might think. Not to be a stick-in-the-mud, but some of us actually find it annoying.

❧❧

Before Valium, there was Mozart.

I say this with no disrespect, but in awe, actually, of the calming power of his music. I listen to Mozart constantly. I listen to the symphonies, piano concerti, sonatas, and quartets. I swear by this music as much for what it gives as for what it takes away. An hour of Mozart can leave one feeling renewed, anchored, at peace. It can also put one to sleep.

The snooze factor is one of those topics people don't discuss. It's shameful, it seems, as if the sheer force of the music should diminish the often-larger forces of exhaustion and fatigue. This isn't logic—just old-fashioned snobbery.

But the facts speak for themselves: look around any concert hall and you'll see pinstriped suits, in fifty-dollar seats, taking very expensive naps.

Philistines, you say?

Perhaps.

More likely, they're soldiers of the nine-to-five grind, thankful that the music is operating at a therapeutic dose. Boredom is not necessarily the culprit. Often the ailment is stress, and the music, with its soothing tones and rhythms, is simply restful.

Nor does this insult Mozart.

Truth is, some of the greatest pleasures put us to sleep. A hearty feast, whether for belly or ears, can be a tiring event.

Still the music has other powers when one is more alert. I often pay bills to Piano Concerto No. 14, water plants to the Flute Quartet in D, and clean house to the "Jupiter" Symphony. The music overrides the droning task at hand and elevates my mood. It has a permeating healthful effect as if I were breathing clear mountain air.

To me, this just argues the case for Mozart's genius, with his power to cheer us up, or down, accordingly. Before Prozac, as well, there was Mozart.

Unlike some people who listen to music while they work or read, my aging brain demands a quieter balance. I listen to Mozart as background, foreground, and everything in between—as an activity itself, a palliative to various tasks, a sideline to puttering around the house. But put on the "Prague" Symphony while I read or work, and my mind derails. I find myself reading the same passage over and over like a broken record, trying to make sense of it. Mozart takes over every time.

Reserving Mozart for "pure" listening is like restricting one's intake of fresh air. It's there for the breathing, if one's nose isn't too high off the ground.

⁂

In the annals of medical conditions, the common cold gets no respect. It's prosaic and dull and, as its name suggests, it's so thoroughly common that we overlook its finer points.

Judging by the television ads, cold sufferers are a miserable lot—pajama-clad sad sacks just waiting for their pills to kick in. They appear to have a single role in life—that of cold sufferer—and all other functions get put on hold. The common cold is portrayed as a full-time job, albeit unpaid, from which employees would rather be laid off.

In reality, though, the common cold rarely affords such luxury. For most of us, there's no way to be heavy-lidded in PJs at the office. The show must go on, and so it does. But not without a few glitches.

Consider the facts: A well-clogged head makes for a foggy brain. Information computes slowly, and not always accurately. So it was that a friend's description of "drinking glasses" registered in my stuffed-up head as a type of eyewear. The thought was mercifully brief, but it did, alas, occur.

When the brain finally clears, that's when the voice goes. One may actually feel better, but sound considerably worse. Which may account for the odd syncopation between one's symptoms and the sympathy they evoke.

The public face of a cold tends to lag a day or two behind. One looks and sounds worse after the fact. This truism makes for a dearth of sympathy when one wants it, and an excess after it's due.

"It sounds like you're straining your voice," people might suggest. Truth is, your scratchy voice is straining their ears. All the while, you're on the mend but for the way you sound.

And what etiquette applies to the common cold?

Heavy breathing of any kind is bad form in the workplace. Coworkers want you quarantined, and wish you had stayed at home. Though you share that wish, there are deadlines to meet and clients to appease. So you're there, coughing and sneezing, allegedly for the greater good.

In the end, this may contribute to the zigzag course that colds often take. It's not a linear path that the common cold follows. More often, it improves or worsens of its own accord, defying the schedule you've assigned it.

By the time you're done with the cold, it's not always done with you. It may just be starting to wreak its havoc on those nearby—

your colleagues, spouse, and kids. Consider this a form of insurance that you won't truly part with it for a while.

Ultimately, those beleaguered folks in the ads might have the right idea. The one-note cold, with its focus on pure misery, is the way to go. Everything else seems doomed to nose its way back into your life.

∾⁊⁊⁊∾

When my favorite doctor decided to retire, he sent a letter to his patients. He thanked everyone for their kindness over the years, said how much he'd enjoyed serving us, and offered a list of physicians.

Frankly, the news came as something of a shock. Dr. Merrick, as I'll call him, was the physician I saw some thirty years ago for my precollege physical. To my eighteen-year-old eyes, he was a small, serious man of parental vintage, ageless and bald. During the three decades that I saw him, he looked exactly the same—only now, this Harvard-trained doc was no longer forty.

I reacted to the news in stages. I was at first surprised and curious (how old is he, anyway?); then disappointed; and finally, grateful that I'd had the good fortune to know the benefits of real, old-fashioned medical care. After a routine exam, Dr. Merrick would hand-write a note to each patient, detailing the results of any x-rays or tests. This high-powered modest man did everything but make house calls.

Thirty years with one doctor is a virtual lifetime in today's world of health care. I now had to find a new internist who would hold up favorably to this dinosaur standard of doctoring.

I phoned Dr. Merrick's office to talk with Ann, the secretary who'd been there for years. I said how sorry I was that the doctor was leaving, and asked whether he had any specific plans. Indeed, the doctor planned to continue with his research at the hospital; it was just time to close the practice. I then asked how other people were taking the news. Patients had been calling with a range of responses—disappointment, appreciation, well-wishing. Some clearly took the news to heart, as if they should have been consulted first. "How dare he leave!" was the apparent sentiment. Then came an onslaught of peeved, discourteous calls from patients who felt displaced. How could Dr. Merrick inconvenience them like that?

According to Ann, the litany of hostile, self-absorbed calls was so constant, even from otherwise polite people, that it nearly became the norm. Bad manners had become an equal opportunity affliction, with no apparent cure. As it turns out, a sense of entitlement is common among patients. I discovered this recently as I was booking an appointment with another physician. Susan, the secretary, told me of the calls she had fielded that morning. One woman had called with a sore throat, needing an appointment. Susan squeezed her in that day for a brief visit, but the woman insisted on a full hour.

Then there was the patient who had never seen the doctor, but demanded an immediate appointment, claiming she had had a pain for the last three months. Since the doctor was fully booked, Susan gave her two options: go to the emergency room, or schedule an office visit for the following week.

The woman hung up.

Perhaps it should come as no surprise that people behave with their doctors the way they do in traffic, in crowds, in so many places these days. Still it's no less disconcerting.

﹏﹏

We've all heard horror stories of medical care gone awry. Then there's the occasional antidote—the feel-good scenario that transports one to an earlier time. Last week I was fighting off a head cold when a cough settled firmly in my chest. Although I was out and about, I was becoming wheezy and short of breath, and thought I'd give my doctor a call. It was early evening, after hours, and my own doc was unavailable. The person who phoned me back was the on-call physician for the practice, a man I'd never met. I described my symptoms, he asked some questions, we quickly got to the issue at hand: I have asthma and wanted to avert complications. Uncertain as to which drug would best supplement my usual regimen, he offered to open the office the next morning to see me.

"On a Saturday?" I asked, obviously taken aback.

He suggested a time and we agreed to meet.

When I arrived for the appointment, he greeted me at the door, looking for all the world as if it were a workday, bowtie and all. This small, dapper man, well into his seventies, moved briskly, with authority. We walked down several corridors to his office.

Sitting on the couch, yellow pad in hand, he asked a host of questions. Fever? Appetite? Any unusual rash or joint pain?

After a thorough exam, he transmitted a prescription to my local pharmacy. He then asked how I got to the appointment. Looking at my address, he offered to drive me to CVS on his way home.

Let's put this in perspective: at a time when our health care system is all but broken, I'm sitting with a doctor who has never met me before, on a Saturday when the office is closed, and he'll double as transportation, if needed, so I can pick up new meds.

Maybe he missed the memo that physicians don't conduct themselves this way in the new millennium—and that those who did gave it up in the second half of the last century. Nor is he a country doctor, schooled in the old, rustic ways. His office is downtown in a city hospital.

The good news is that this doctor is also an educator who teaches medical residents. One can only hope that some of the future docs in his charge will emulate his rare breed of dedication.

I thanked the doctor for his time, his kindness and, unbeknownst to him, for the full-blown strangeness of the whole encounter. I then drove to CVS, picked up the medicine, went home, and went to bed.

Next morning, Sunday, I check my voice mail and find that the doctor has left a message:

"Hi, Ms. Silverman. I just wanted to make sure you're okay. If you're worried or things aren't going well, just page me."

CHAPTER SIX: OBSESSIONS

Forty years ago, I was an avid philatelist. I collected stamps with a passion and single-mindedness rare for a twelve-year-old. Every week or so, I'd go down to the nearby stamp shop, trade issues at the local stamp club, and occasionally sell an item or two. My "customers" were other like-minded twelve-year-olds. Whenever my parents would travel abroad, I'd give them lists of plate blocks and mint sheets that I deemed essential to my collection. Dutifully, they returned with whatever they could find.

Recently, I stumbled upon my forty-year-old stamp collection in the basement. And with it, I unearthed an entire world of comfort and curiosity, tidiness and joy.

The world was a different place then. There were whole nations and territories that figured prominently in my collection—Basutoland, Ifni, Württemberg—that have since been renamed, absorbed, or swallowed up by other countries. If England didn't quite rule the world, it certainly had its share of obscure islands and outposts. All of this was neatly chronicled in crisp sets of stamps, variously hued and denominated.

Every day after homework, I would sit at my desk mesmerized, magnifier in hand, poring over new stamps. Some would end up in files, others in manila envelopes, the worthier specimens displayed in albums. To look at my collection today is to see major world events portrayed in miniature: the birth of the United Nations, the invention of electricity, the printing press—all were commemorated on postage stamps. Sometimes a cause was global, such as the 1960s campaign against malaria, which generated postal issues from Mexico, France, China, and Kuwait. Eventually stamps would turn Whitmanesque and celebrate themselves. Few nations are exempt from commemorating their own postage.

One of the great wonders of stamp collecting is the way it allows one to encounter the world. For all their historic value, stamps could well be considered revisionist. While they provide glimpses of war and upheaval, the evidence is often sanitized. Postage stamps, like politics, can be little banners of disinformation—images that a nation chooses to project. As collectors, we take these well-pruned images and array them neatly in albums for viewing. If the messiness of life gets tamed and dwarfed in the process, those albums are no less lovely because of it. And there's the rub.

The nearly meditative, solitary quiet that attends the act of stamp collecting is decidedly unlike the state of the world. It provides a peaceful entree to parts of the globe that simply aren't. So, as a twelve-year-old, I observed men with beards and turbans on various foreign postage, for instance, and I would note whether or not I found them handsome. Whether these same men, kings and leaders of their nations, were brutal or oppressive was never the point. I collected stamps as pure pieces of geography, of commerce and beauty. Politics had no place. And as such, my young philatelist's view of the world was remarkably free of bias.

Historically, stamps have enabled people to communicate by mail. Long before the digital age, people hand-wrote letters, stamped an envelope, and their words would travel to another town or country. Stamps themselves were always miniature works of art—engravings, screen prints, drawings—that offered a window on the world.

From where I sat, they more than delivered.

❧ ❧

If you've ever eaten a single-serve cup of yogurt or applesauce with a standard teaspoon, you know the problem: the spoon often dwarfs the container, looming in its disproportion. Of course, it fits inside, and can serve the contents adequately, but it's not a pretty sight. It's the wrong tool for the task, like a shovel when a scoop would do.

After eating, you confront another side of the issue, especially if the spoon is metal: lacking ballast, an empty aluminum or plastic cup simply falls on its side, caving to the weight of the teaspoon, as if to declare an end to your snack.

The spoon is a mighty implement with a long and venerable history. It has withstood the advent of soups, stews, and every other food that ever required stirring. Surely the portable snack poses little challenge to such a sturdy tradition. The issue, then, is not the spoon exactly, but its configuration. Size matters. Trying to coax a food from a snack-sized container requires a snack-sized spoon— one whose bowl and handle are scaled down to the task, whose materials are equally modest.

Picture a teaspoon, reduced by a third.

Such a spoon arrived in my kitchen a couple of years ago when a friend thought to share a discovery. She had stumbled upon some sleek plastic spoons—small flatware that was several notches above disposable. Truth is, my friend and I share a lifelong fondness for small, well-designed flatware, and she correctly assumed that I would enjoy this little spoon. The spoon appeared to be just the right size and weight for mustard or other condiments. That is, until I ventured into the world of portable snacks, and realized it had higher aspirations.

Over time, that lone mini-spoon served hundreds of snacks, repeatedly landed in the disposal and rubbish, and still managed to survive. It was time to raise the inevitable question: Where did my friend find this spoon?

"Berlin," she replied. She offered to pick up more spoons on her next trip to Germany.

Berlin?

Surely there were similar spoons closer to home. And so my mission began.

I Googled "spoons" and checked various sources for flatware. Among the possibilities were spoons for fishing; spoons sold in large volume for restaurants; replacements for the lost or damaged pieces in one's silver service. There was a museum of spoons, a blog by the same name, and firms that sell souvenir spoons.

I waded through yet more spoons—with cartoon logos, with rubber grips, with angled bowls or handles. And there it was: something that looked remarkably like the small designer plastic spoon that came from Germany. It went by the utilitarian name of Disposable Baby Feeding Utensils, pack of thirty spoons, for $4.95. I ordered two packages—one for me, one for my friend.

Granted, the new spoons lack the cachet that comes with exotic origin or European flight. They're not as firm or substantial as the original. But all things considered, they're a plausible stand-in. For less than twenty cents each, they solve a problem that conventional teaspoons have yet to match.

෴

They're at it again. My neighbors up the street are having their daily confab, standing at the edge of the driveway, analyzing the snow mass, studying the angle of the drifts. These two men own houses side by side, and they share an adjoining driveway. What's obvious is that they share much more. To observe their handiwork in all its phases, from strategy (where to put the snow) through execution (actually shoveling it), is to witness the soul of male bonding. No sport or tech device could flex so many muscles.

At the moment, we're recovering from yet another storm, with a fresh pile of snow. To the naked eye, my neighbors' lot appears to be neatly shoveled. That, of course, won't keep these men from rearranging the private universe they've created. And so, they're shoveling again, without any obvious or new reason to shovel.

Indeed, my neighbors give new meaning to the term "microclimate." Their driveway is the only outdoor surface within miles that has been wholly liberated from snow. It is an odd spectacle to behold.

What is the satisfaction, I wonder, in a perfectly manicured, snowless driveway? It's true that, amid the unending whiteness, asphalt has never looked so good. But it is, at bottom, asphalt. A dusting of white, a ragged edge or two, would humanize the whole effect.

Which may be exactly what my neighbors want to avoid. With their countless shovels for every type and texture of snow, they micro-manage their own weather. When a storm arrives, they dig into their arsenal of winter weaponry and launch an all-out assault.

This is where my respect for this duo reaches its pinnacle: too often, the trick to shoveling is outwitting the plows. We shovel ourselves out—they plow us back in. It's a perennial battle of home-owners versus road crews. And the little guy rarely wins.

Except in the case of my neighbors. In a brilliant counter-attack, they have created their own perfectly placed six-foot drift, beyond the reach of even the most ambitious plow. They have become homeowner and road crew all in one.

It's a high maintenance operation my neighbors run, what with their constant plotting and tinkering, their endless analysis of snows past and present. The logical next step for these guys would be to think ahead—to divert the white stuff before it ever lands.

❧ ☙

One of the first things one notices about the Berkshires in western Massachusetts is the landscape—how old and tall and green are the wooded areas, how serious and manicured are the man-made ones. Inn after inn along the road has the distinctively cropped lawn, rounded hedges, and lush gardens that suggest a level of maintenance that's never-ending. If a property is large and compli-cated enough, with sufficient acreage and imagination, there's no way around it. Not surprisingly, one of the dominant sounds in this setting is that of competing power mowers.

If one listens carefully, there is always a lawn mower to be heard, if not seen, during daytime.

At the inn where I was staying, I sat reading on the patio one afternoon as the grounds were being kept up—a succession of chores that went on for hours. First came the hand mower, then the seated power mower, then a tractor with a separate wagon attached.

Ted, the owner of the inn, served as groundskeeper, manning all of the machinery himself. He had obviously gone through this routine hundreds of times before, rounding the property with each machine, riding in smaller concentric circles, nearing the edges of a grove of trees, or rose bushes, then fanning out to another part of the estate. He drove the tractor slightly too fast, as if the added speed might give an edge to an activity that had all but lost interest.

As I watched the procession of machinery circling the landscape, I noticed that nothing changed. After two rounds of mowing, the grass was cut. It didn't get shorter, or cleaner, or more finished-looking with each successive round—it was simply more mowed.

Yet Ted was undeterred. After power mowing, he would mount the tractor and trace the same stretch of land three, four, five times—I lost count. At some point, I simply marveled at the odd mechanics of this groundskeeping operation, the over and over of it, for no apparent reason. Perhaps the machinery picked up clippings that would otherwise mar the landscape. But the shape and height of the lawn—coddled, cropped, and shaved as it was—remained the same. If there was some improvement to be gained from all this repetition, it wasn't visible to the naked eye.

When, two days later, the entire exercise was repeated on the identical swath of land, I began to wonder just what it was I was witnessing. Was this a case of dull blades causing an amazing display of inefficiency? Or perhaps it was wishful lawn care, whereby one could mow more now in hopes of mowing less later.

Then I saw Ted circling a pear tree with his rig, ducking under a branch, and turning to watch the wagon follow his lead. It was the perfect metaphor: he looked like a dog chasing its tail, going round and round.

Had I simply passed by and seen a man using a lawn mower or tractor, I would have known what I was seeing. They are the common tools of lawn care, and straightforward ones, at that. But as the process thickened and grew dense with repetition, I became less certain of what this was.

At some stage, of course, Ted was indeed mowing the lawn. But by the end of the day, the concentric circles he drew in the grass were as much his own as those he created with the machines.

❧ ❧

"Paper-thin" is the term for this sliver of sheet that I hold in my hand. It is standard laser paper, of good weight, medium smoothness, with a brightness rating of ninety-one. It is designed for the laser printers so many of us use, and equally suited for copying. It is the copying part–that one might wish to duplicate something on a page–that is the tip-off to those who would make our future paperless.

I want this sheet in my hand–this sliver of words and images; smooth, bright surface that I can wrinkle, fold, or pocket, pick up and put down; this opening to the world.

A world without paper would be a place of diminishing returns–no notes or memos, no "call home at 6," no "to-do" lists posted on the fridge. A world without paper would be a place without a sense of itself, a street without a sign. And as its inhabitants, we would arguably be lost. "Lost" is perhaps an exaggeration, though not by much.

There are whole generations of screen readers afoot, digital natives who take in words from a smartphone, whose dealings with text and images are essentially the same. Words, videos, graphics are all viewed on a screen. There is none of the texture of old-fashioned reading–the dog-eared pages, underlined passages, bindings that open to the spot where we nodded off into sleep.

Paper is the surface from which we traditionally read, the form that holds thought, the tray offering food. Without it, there is a hunger that goes unfed. It's true that large quantities of paper are cumbersome. They take up space and presume squatter's rights. Who doesn't have some pile of newspapers, or work documents, or catalogs—some mounting stash of paper for which there is no proper place other than wherever it is at the moment?

And this seems perfectly fitting: Were it all neatly stored on some hard drive, we would lack the sense of intrusion that these papers impart. Paper is intrusive—there's no denying it. If we welcome the intrusion—the sense of place, of permanence, of rectangles piled in space—we can glimpse the breadth of how paper fits in our daily life, its textures everywhere.

Even the lingo of the paper trade tells the story. Paper is measured in "grain" and "substance," words with body and character. A screen, by contrast, is measured in inches and pixels, pieces of words struggling to become whole on a display. When they do appear, they can vanish just as quickly, receding into the annals of memory. Though I've come to trust technology to a surprising degree, it's my own fingers that I distrust: "delete" is a button I can't press on a printed page, and good thing, at that.

Whoever envisions a paperless society places his trust in the air, for the vision is one of invisibility, without texture or touch. A virtual world, where sense is made formless, and words lack a permanent home, is a place where meanings can shift like the wind.

The hunger for paper is more than a wish to touch some smooth, or grainy, or coated surface. It is the need to touch something real.

꿰 껯

It's a new variation on an old theme. The family returns from vacation, thoroughly exhausted. Not that they did all that much running around, or saw that many sights; it was the sheer amount of listening that wore them out.

"She has so many opinions!" my friend exclaimed of her sister-in-law. Just name a topic, and some newly-formed stance was at the ready. Nor was any subject too remote. Apparently, there was a tacit rule that everything requires a point of view, carefully considered or not. It hadn't occurred to the sister-in-law that abstinence might be a worthy stance—to simply abstain from forming, and sharing, yet one more viewpoint.

Abstaining from an opinion is decidedly an opinion itself. Indeed, the realization that one might pick and choose issues to ponder, rather than mulling over every item that crosses one's path, has serious merit. Not to mention how liberating it can be.

I came to this revelation not long ago when some news item caught my eye. I recall thinking about the story at hand and wondering where I stood. Then right there, smack in the middle of the process, I found myself in the act of forming an opinion. Like so many opinions, this one was extraneous and unsolicited—the mind grappling with a concept, musing about some question or theory, coming down on one side or another. It was a purely idle exercise, of zero consequence.

That, of course, is the beauty of inquisitiveness, of looking around the nooks and crannies of an idea.

Without it, the world would be a simpler place, and duller, to be sure. Yet taken to the extreme, inquisitiveness has its faults. Devising a point of view for every issue that comes down the pike, as if there were some syllabus of required topics on which one had to opine, is tiring—not to mention pointless. Better, it seems, to understand the role of opinions and where they may, or may not, serve some use.

In social settings, for instance, it helps to be able to converse on a variety of topics—say, movies or sports, or other subjects of common interest. Opinions are a form of social currency, a ticket of entry.

Too many opinions coming from one mouth, however, can have a deafening effect, like so much droning. It's the relentless sister-in-law syndrome.

Or consider the fact that there are certain subjects that you don't really grasp, that hold no interest for you—say, astrophysics. It's an area where your opinion won't matter a whit. This is a great leveler—to realize that many of our views are basically diversions, of little use beyond themselves. If anything, they're more like primal assertions: I breathe, therefore I opine.

Of course, there's always the fallback stance, which one shouldn't hesitate to employ. "I don't know" is as fresh and startling a statement as one is likely to hear, stunning for its sheer novelty. At a time when information is so ubiquitous, when people are bloated with points of view, "I don't know" can be a real showstopper. It holds up well as a declaration of opinions you've decided not to form.

❧ ❧

I was in a hurry. I had just come from the post office and was rushing back to the car, when something caught my eye. I turned around and walked back three stores to an Oriental rug shop that had closed for the night. Far behind the storefront, hanging on the back wall, was the object of my distraction—an earthy brick-red rug with a geometric pattern. I reached into my briefcase and grabbed a notepad and pen.

"I'd like to buy the red rug on the back wall," my note said. "Will call Monday." I signed my name, and shoved the note under the front door.

On the ride home, I alternated between imagining this exquisite rug in my living room, and thinking I had gone off the beam. I had just committed to buying something I could barely see, for a price I didn't know, from a store I had never been to. All in the space of three minutes. This wasn't an impulse purchase, exactly; it was more like an alien encounter. I didn't know whether to be startled more by the sense of awe that I felt in viewing this beautiful thing, or by the urgency of my desire to own it. The rug was mine: I had only to wait until Monday to claim it.

Over the weekend, I began to fret about all of the proper rational concerns. Was the rug $300, or $3,000, and what was it worth, anyway? Did I know enough about Oriental rugs to assess its quality and condition? And how big was it?

On a wall, it was hard to gauge the size and how it would fit in the place I envisioned it.

By the time Monday rolled around, I had worked up a hearty ambivalence, worrying about the practical details, and hoping I would return to the shop and feel nothing. I felt so powerless in the grip of this material desire that my only hope of mastery would be to walk away empty-handed. If the price was right, though, I knew I could live quite happily feeling powerless.

I called the shop that morning and sheepishly introduced myself to the owner. "I'm the one who left the note about the red rug," I said.

The owner, of course, was pleased to hear from me—the note, at least, wasn't a crank and, surely, he had never sold a rug with so little effort. We spoke for a few minutes and he confirmed my worst fear: the price was right—I could afford to feel powerless.

When I returned to the store, the rug was no less beautiful. If anything, it may have been more so because I was seeing it, for the first time, up close. There was no question in my mind, though I fabricated several to appease myself. As the discussion was winding down, the owner cautioned, "You should buy the rug only if it speaks to you."

Clearly it had spoken.

It is now fifteen years that I've owned the rug, happily and without regret. Thankfully, the experience of buying it, the grip and pull and urgency, have never resurfaced in any other shopping foray. Had this become routine, some serious therapy would have been in order.

Instead I have come to view this experience as a variant of love-at-first-sight—a simple, lower species, perhaps, but with many of the attendant emotions. I think it's possible, even useful, to love certain objects and things for the sheer uncomplicated pleasure they give. It's not like loving another person; it's different and simpler, and lacks some obvious components. But as a friend once noted, "How many things in life can give so much pleasure, and ask so little in return?"

Consider, too, the economics. Spread out over fifteen years, the cost of my rug is quite modest, and it only decreases with time. So, despite the old adage, perhaps there really is a free lunch. If so, it's one helluva long feast.

CHAPTER SEVEN: HE SAID, SHE SAID

Old-fashioned and folksy are two of the signature traits of a country store. If you're going to sell penny candy and wind-up clocks, then a certain old-time charm would seem to befit the enterprise. So it is that The Vermont Country Store hams it up in its vintage-style catalogs, promoting the hallmarks of Vermont-ness.

Several years back in the firm's catalog, then-proprietor Lyman Orton expounded on the theme of "Vermont Men and Pronouns." Said Orton, "Many male Vermonters have a disconcerting, although somewhat amusing, habit of speaking of their wives or girl-friends in pronoun terms, out of the blue without the context of setting."

There you are, chatting about, say, sports or food when, apropos of nothing, a man might offer, "She had her car fixed this morning." She, we're supposed to glean, is obviously and unmistakably his wife, beyond need of naming. Orton further speculates that this referential tic may date back to an earlier time and place when everyone knew everyone else.

Many women know precisely the habit of which Orton speaks. We laugh and shake our heads about it. Ah, men! But it's not just Vermonters who use this shorthand. This is a distinctly male quirk, lacking in regional charm. Indeed, some would say that the unan-chored use of "she" is simply rude and charmless.

Not to mention that it's wildly presumptuous. When "she" crops up in conversation, out of nowhere, and with no prior reference, listeners may be more than a little puzzled. Suddenly their role has turned to that of mind reader.

But the basic problem is less social or political than linguis-tic. Stripped of antecedents, pronouns float in a sea of vagueness. These, it, those—all assume prior reference to something; without them, listeners are left to fill in the blanks. Other pronouns fare even worse. Try inserting the word "they" into a conversation, without identifying who "they" are, and you set the stage for polarization. Similarly, the use of "we," without establishing who "we" are, can suggest a sort of clubbiness.

In the matter of "she," the lack of any previously named woman can be downright confounding—call it the hanging chad of marital monikers.

Back to the catalog.

In defense of the minimalist approach, Orton concludes, "We Vermonters are infamously frugal and we extend that frugality to words."

Fine. No need to spring even for extra syllables.

Just start with the ones—like Sue, Ann, Jane, or Peg—that actually name the wife in question.

***

It was a quick cellphone exchange to confirm evening plans: "Feeling okay?" I asked.

"Fine, except for some hot flashes," came the reply on speakerphone.

"Time for some girl talk!" I quipped. And with that, we hung up.

What I failed to realize was that our exchange wasn't private—that six others were in on the joke, and all of them male.

"Girl talk," it turns out, is a relative term, no longer the sole domain of the reigning estrogen set. If you're a man undergoing treatment for prostate cancer, you may feel perfectly at home with the term. Such was the case with my friend, Brian, and his gang of six. All were sitting in a hospital anteroom, awaiting their daily radiation treatment.

Like many of the women he knows, Brian, at sixty-two, is taking hormones. In his case, though, they're part of his prostate cancer therapy, to suppress testosterone. Still, he's enjoying the new status his treatment has conferred upon him. No, he hasn't morphed into a sensitive guy who wants to talk about feelings. Frankly, he's always been that way. But he's gaining a certain empathy that comes from being an accidental interloper.

Brian knows how lucky he is. He observes one of the guys in his group whose internal thermostat is totally out of whack, who routinely drenches his clothes. Another has been taking hormones for two years now. He warns of their cumulative effects—that Brian's few months of treatment are a mere flash in the hormonal pan.

Women may have a genetic claim to hot flashes, but seeing other men in the process has handed Brian an unexpected mirror. His "adventure," as he calls it, goes beyond hot flashes, though. Suddenly he seems to know countless men who have, or recently had, prostate cancer. Listening to him, one might conclude that the disease is nearly epidemic. Truth is, now that it's surfacing on Brian's own radar, he's seeing it everywhere. Call it a coincidence of noticing.

Then there's the big picture of Brian's day-to-day life. To look at him, one sees a dark, strapping man with a full head of hair, the picture of health. In addition to his day job, he tutors a student or two, socializes regularly, has a live-in girlfriend, and otherwise leads a full and active life. Looking at him, one would never guess that he's had a heart attack, or years of back trouble, or that he's currently undergoing cancer treatment. Remarkably, he shows little wear and tear, few telltale signs of the medical odyssey he's been on.

"So it was just another routine day with radiation?" I joked when we got together.

"No, it was better than that," he said. "One of my more difficult students didn't come to class today."

৸৶৶৶

Walgreen's is not the best place for philosophical musing. But there I was, en route to hand creams, when I found myself in the

"Hygiene" aisle. Beside me was a man in his forties, looking decidedly perplexed. He was trying to take in the array of feminine products—scented and unscented; slim, super, and super-plus; with wings and without.

Of course he was confused. Who wouldn't be?

This is not just a "guy thing." Women are no less puzzled by the maze of choices. But this was a man with a mission. He had no list, or other evidence of the instructions he was given. What he had was a determination to get it right. His seriousness was impressive: he studied the products on the shelves as if they had a meaning beyond themselves. Perhaps they did.

Frankly, my chores in this aisle took less time than I actually spent there. I admit to having dawdled. I was interested in this man—not in him personally, but his plight. I liked his diligence—I respected his fear. This was a man with good survival instincts. He knew that arriving home with the wrong product was a bad idea. There would be consequences.

"Dad, you are completely clueless!" his teenage daughter might shout.

Or, if the woman in question was his wife, it might go like this: "Honey, you just never listen."

He would defend himself, only to be challenged by the obvious question: "Then why didn't you ask someone for help?"

I had been in similar situations at the florist's, for instance, where men were shopping. They were debating between two types of flowers, or two different colors, and they wanted a woman's view. I'm always glad to comply, especially if someone has the sense to ask. Granted, it's easier to ask for guidance about flowers than feminine hygiene products. Not only is it less embarrassing; there's less risk of seeming like a stalker. Besides, one stands a better chance of asking the right questions, and thus, getting the right answers.

But the man beside me was in a bind. Whatever he was sent there to get appeared to be missing from the shelves. Alas, he came to Walgreen's for a product, not a biology lesson. What he got instead was a crash course in micro-marketing.

Finally, the man grabbed a box from the shelf and headed for the checkout counter. No doubt, someone was either pleased, or furious, when he arrived home.

           ✎✎

On a recent Friday night, four of us went to a small Mediterranean restaurant whose menu encourages lots of back-and-forth with the waiters. For many of us, items like bronzini and tsoureki require translation, which, in turn, builds a bit of rapport. Our waiter, who resembled New Age musician Yanni, was animated and likable, engaging each of us in small talk while decoding the menu. All was going well until he delivered a basket of bread.

As I recall, the four of us were busily talking, as diners are wont to do, when one of us mentioned the word "gynecologist." The waiter arrived, bread in hand, just in time to overhear.

He didn't simply place the bread on the table and leave. He opted instead for a bit of showboating. His eyebrows jumped. He backed off theatrically, in mock astonishment at what he had just overheard.

Would "podiatrist" have elicited the same response? But never mind.

Our server had broken a cardinal rule of waiting tables—namely, inserting himself into our conversation. Suddenly, he was no longer aiding and abetting our dining experience; he had plunked himself smack in the middle of it.

It was clear that he was being playful and hammy—he meant no disrespect. We all just laughed it off. But somehow that exchange managed to unleash his inner bad boy. He proceeded to tell an off-color joke, with apologies before, during, and after. He allowed as how his boss wouldn't appreciate this sort of humor.

Nor did we.

One wonders how such misguided conduct begins, finds a perch and even a place of employment. True, restaurants have long provided a second stage for underpaid, underworked actors. But that still doesn't account for the oversharing part. For that, one needs only to consider Facebook and the world of social media. There the lines of discretion aren't just blurred; they barely exist. The old 1960s adage, "There's no such thing as strangers, only friends you haven't met," takes on new irony. Nowadays, we have "Facebook friends," which often have as much to do with friendship as, well, the relation between bronzini and gynecologists.

Which gets back to our waiter. It's a fine line that waiters tread when talking with diners. I'm not suggesting that a server's personality be expunged from the exchange—think of the clever waiters who have saved an otherwise dull dinner conversation—only that there's an art to chatting with diners that requires a certain finesse.

Mind you, I like a good risqué joke as much as the next person. But I'd rather hear it in a setting that requires no apology.

✖✖✖

It was 1970 when we first met. I was nineteen; he was about fifty.

Every week we would sit through Student Council meetings—I, a sophomore defender of student rights; he, a faculty advocate of common sense. I liked him right from the start—everything from his three-piece name to his scholarly garb. He was a tweed-and-bowtie sort of guy, a native New Englander who was built like a battleship. Shake his hand and you knew exactly where you stood. Gerrit Hubbard Roelofs was a force to be reckoned with, and reckon we did.

Week after week, we would debate the merits of various student events—which ones to fund, approve, or dismiss. Which campus site would best suit a political rally? How late was too late for a weekend dance?

Roelofs and I agreed in substance on most matters. But left to the details, we would dicker endlessly as if it were sport. I think it was.

The following year, I spent both semesters abroad, paying little attention to my studies. Senior year I returned to pay the consequences: I had yet to fulfill the core curriculum for an English major—I had missed several courses. As a result, there were large gaps that had to be filled before I could pass comprehensive exams at the end of senior year. Unfortunately, my faculty advisor was a man who loved books, not students. He would be of little help.

A few days after returning, I went to see Roelofs. "Welcome back!" he exclaimed, greeting me with his big, battleship hug.

In no time, Roelofs was taking charge of my academic life. First, he offered to become my advisor. He filed the papers and made it official. Next, he outlined my options for coursework, suggesting which combinations made the most sense. Among the courses would be Brit. Lit., a twice-weekly lecture for which Roelofs was well known. This was his forte and my weakest link.

Still there was the problem of my "gaps," for which no single course was the solution. We would invent one: we came up with a list of Great Works, and formalized it as a full-credit independent study. Roelofs agreed to supervise the effort. We would meet twice a week and I would submit eight papers during the term.

"Miss Silverman," Roelofs called out in Brit. Lit. "Can you describe the use of assonance in this sonnet?"

Probably not, I suspect, since my attendance in Brit. Lit. was somewhat less than diligent. His was an early-morning class, mine a late-night schedule. But Roelofs had a plan for this problem, too: on the mornings of his class, he would call to wake me—just a friendly reminder to please show up. Thankfully, he knew not to be offended by my spotty attendance. He knew that, for me, his course was the broccoli in a balanced diet.

The real meal, it turned out, was the tutorial we planned together. There we plowed through *The Faerie Queene, King Lear, Paradise Lost*. I had never encountered great literature in quite this way. We would be discussing some aspect of, say, *Troilus and Criseyde*—some way in which she had slighted him. Roelofs would get so worked up on Troilus's behalf, his eyes would well up, his face turn red. This looming tank of a man would just dissolve at his desk, contemplating Troilus's wounded ego. He made you feel for Troilus in ways you couldn't have imagined.

Come the end of the semester, I submitted my eighth and final paper for the tutorial. Roelofs, in turn, submitted the following idea: he asked me to evaluate my own work and to recommend a grade for the term. He agreed to abide by my decision.

To be, or not to be honest, was never the question. The question was just how honest I was prepared to be.

"For the work I've done," I wrote in the evaluation, "I would give myself an A. But because of the work I didn't do, I would give myself a B. The decision is yours."

And with those words, I threw the ball back into Roelofs's court, having evened-up the score. For the first time, I had admitted what we both knew. He had trusted me to tell the truth; I had trusted him to be fair.

I don't recall which grade Roelofs ultimately submitted. What I recall was the strange joy of the whole exchange—his, mine, the surprise of the encounter.

Looking back twenty-five years later, I have to wonder how this same relationship with its quirky aspects, its morning wake-up calls, would play on campus today. I wonder if Roelofs and I would have become such great friends, or whether we would have been subject to more contemporary scrutiny. Sadly, I suspect both.

CHAPTER EIGHT: BUT WHO'S COUNTING?

I had another encounter today with the math problem. Not my math problem, exactly, but the problem that afflicts a large part of our culture.

It crops up in simple daily transactions like, "Could I have a third of a pound of Swiss cheese?"

This modest request, issued politely at a deli counter, is not a test. Nor is it a trick question. I am not asking for five and a third ounces of cheese (try cutting that, pal!) or a precise .33 on the scale. I'd just like about a third of a pound.

Granted, this may not be the most commonly sought-after amount; it is, however, measurable. Or so you would think.

"A third of a pound," one deli assistant puzzled. "Is that more, or less, than a half pound?"

Another asked, "Is that the same as three tenths of a pound?"

Well, sort of.

When variations of this response started to become the norm, I began taking a different tack. I would ask for five or six ounces. To the mathematically-impaired, however, five ounces isn't much help. When the scale metes out portions in hundredths of a pound, five ounces still requires some thought–more, perhaps, than the cheese warrants, but certainly more than the deli crew is prepared to give.

So lately I've adopted a more user-friendly approach. Before placing my order, I look at the scale and do the arithmetic myself. If the scale calculates hundredths of a pound, so will I: "I'd like about .30 of a pound." If it measures ounces, I'll stick with tried-and-true fractions, but with a twist: "I'd like somewhere between a quarter pound and a half pound of Swiss cheese." The imprecision is deliberate; it gets me closer to the amount I want, without venturing into higher math.

One might conclude from these episodes that I'm dealing with a specific population, in a single location, and that this picture will not be playing soon at a deli near you.

Don't count on it.

Truth is, the delis in question are both urban and suburban, gourmet and not-so. The counter help are of every stripe and color, both sexes, and with varying numbers of pierced parts.

Judging from the behind-the-counter chatter, some are apparently college students. Not insignificantly, one of the delis is located in a town that boasts one of the top public school systems in the nation.

If there's a common denominator here, it is age. The offending parties are invariably twenty-somethings. In time, of course, this means they will become thirty-somethings and forty-somethings, and their own children may wind up doing a stint behind a deli counter. By then, perhaps, a new generation of counter help will be spared the task of calculating at all: I will speak directly to a scale which, in turn, will translate the amount of cheese to be cut.

Until then, I may give up on all of this measuring stuff. Instead I'll just ask for a medium hunk of cheese—sliced, please.

❧ ❦

It was a Saturday night. We were meeting friends for dinner at a favorite haunt. The four of us ordered simple fare—pizza for two, a sandwich, grilled tuna. We talked about everything from politics to food, a new computer, a very old dog. Then this unlikely notion: Sharon described how she and Jim had been talking the other night, when he asked whether one could get a rebate for lost time. A decade before, Jim had gone through a messy divorce that, by his calculation, stole five years from his life.

So we batted around the idea. If a rebate were available, would it take material form, maybe cash?

Or perhaps it would reclaim time for some later chapter of one's life.

Would it serve as a form of revenge, relief, extrication, or something else?

And who, or what, would issue the rebate, anyway?

The conversation roamed from one quirky premise to the next. There's nothing like a good metaphysical musing to spice up a meal.

Meanwhile, as we chewed over these contemplations, our dinner arrived. Part way through my tuna, I noticed something odd—a chicken bone, gray and bare, perched near the fish. The fact of this discovery might have alarmed me, had I not already fastened on something worse—namely, how long it took me to spot it. We summoned the waitress, who promptly removed the offending plate. A second round of grilled tuna arrived soon after.

That errant chicken bone derailed our discussion, leading us into earthier, more comical terrain. We never did settle the rebate question, nor, perhaps, was it meant to be settled. Yet when the waitress returned later with our check, she noted that there was no charge for my meal. One of us, at least, was getting a rebate. In its way, our dinner had achieved an unintended symmetry.

Of course, no amount of free meals, mine or Jim's, could pay a man back for five rancid years of life. Still they can have a buoying effect. They're momentary offsets, small bits of justice that sometimes turn up.

❧⁂☙

I can remember learning the multiplication tables as a kid. I liked the clear sequence of numbers, their calm, orderly pattern. I also liked the certainty they afforded. Two times two was always four—there was no room for haggling. The tables, we were told, were an essential part of life, a way to shore up young minds.

Many years later, however, my nine-year-old niece set me straight. The multiplication tables, she advised, were obsolete. Why bother to learn them when you could use a calculator instead?

"Yes," I countered, "but what happens when the batteries die?"

"You borrow a friend's calculator," she replied.

So much for the preparation of young minds. Preparedness is not what it used to be.

Like many people, I've long had an emergency pack in the trunk of my car. It contains the usual supplies—flashlight, first aid kit, booster cables, plus an assortment of winter driving aids. I also keep some emergency food on hand—vacuum-packed snacks that would be fresh when, say, a flat tire might preempt a legitimate meal. And I have the requisite change of clothes for the emergency that lasts longer than one wants to contemplate. In a word, I'm generally prepared.

Over time, I've also been lucky. No real emergency has ever come up, thus leaving most of my supplies idle and unopened. So, when I traded in my ten-year-old car earlier this year, I was surprised to survey the contents of my trunk. There were multiples of everything—four ice scrapers, three flashlights, two first aid kits. On first glance, one might assume that I thought more is better. I don't. Truth is, I'd tossed these items into the trunk, having forgotten their predecessors.

If I seemed over-prepared, it was just a façade. Forgetfulness wears many masks. Meanwhile, the spare clothes smelled of oil, rubber, and gas—fine for a service station, less so for a human.

The sorry state of my decade-old supplies got me thinking. What would I transfer to the trunk of my new car, and what would I delete altogether?

The question recalled news stories one hears about day hikers lost in the woods. In place of emergency gear, some carry only cell phones. I wondered how many drivers might do the equivalent—dispense with their car emergency kits, in favor of this digital panacea.

Then I thought back to my niece and the multiplication tables, and the veneer of confidence that her calculator had fostered. Not that a cell phone wouldn't be useful in an emergency; but the ability to think through a problem, or shovel one's way out of a snowbank, might be more so.

※≈※

They are standing by the front window of the shop, haggling over an antique Windsor chair. "How much does it cost?" the woman asks, rubbing its burnished arm, looking for a price.

"How much do you want to pay?" the dealer replies.

But the woman refuses to take the bait. If she goes first, she falls into the gray-space of not knowing—of playing the game too high and over-paying; or too low and, at once, insulting the dealer and foiling the exchange. It is his chair, his call—let him name the price.

When she buys shoes or dishes, after all, no one asks what she'd like to pay; the price is declared and known. It's the cost of doing business. Her opinion isn't sought; no one inquires about the hierarchy of what she wants, or is willing to pay, or how high she'll ultimately go. She hands over her money; they give her the goods.

Yet the antiques dealer is asking the most basic, unknowable question: "What's it worth to you?" he asks in the parlance.

He is, of course, banking on the beauty of the chair to sell itself, on the woman's eye to envision it at home, on the power of objects to insinuate themselves into our lives. He is asking what piece of her wallet she's willing to spare; she is pondering how much pleasure she's buying in return. But how can she know what this chair may come to mean?

How do we measure meaning?

In the world of commerce, the measures are clear—a price tag, an hourly rate, a clock on the wall. "Time is money," the saying goes, and even the clock has its price. We may disagree with that price, finding a gap between the amount charged and the value we would place on it. By virtue of a price tag, a store sets the meaning of its goods. By leaving empty-handed, so do we.

In our daily contacts, we often think the measures are clear even when they're not. "I'll take sugar in my coffee," millions of us say every day. But is that one sugar, or two, or some other amount?

So, too, we say things to one another and expect the meaning will be understood. "You just can't imagine how much this means to me," a friend says. And she may well be right. It may not be simply rhetorical. Between friends, there are no literal price tags, just metaphorical ones—invitations issued, thoughts shared, gestures made. How they all add up for one person may not equate with another's tally. Each of us sees the world differently, gleans different things from it.

In the absence of clocks and price tags, we need other guideposts to mark the trail. It's hard enough to take a measure of meaning in one's own life; harder, still, to ponder it in others. To tell someone that she can't imagine how much something means is like the product without a price tag—the woman in the store haggling over a chair. It's a guessing game, of sorts—a form of hide-and-seek.

It is far better to show one's hand—to tell the truth with its prickly edges, its questions at the core. In so doing, one risks becoming equals.

❧ ❧

It was a frigid winter night, in the single digits. Given the choice, one would have stayed home. I happened to be on my way to a meeting, driving with the heat pumped up. As I slowed down for a set of lights, something caught my eye. A man was pacing the traffic island, wearing a sandwich board with his life story posted on it.

I had maybe two minutes before the light would change, so I glossed over the fine print and pulled out the headlines: Vietnam vet, homeless, needs place to sleep.

If his story wasn't exactly new, his packaging was certainly different. What I noticed at a distance wasn't the man himself, but the writing on the board. He told his tale in large, even block letters, the kind that won penmanship awards in school. At the top of the board, in boldface, above his story, were the hard facts. He needed forty-five dollars for the night, as I recall, and he marked each dollar he'd received, to keep track. By the time I pulled up to the lights, he was more than halfway home.

When it comes to charity, I give at the office, as the saying goes. But as I watched this graying vet work his traffic island, selling his story to a captive row of cars, my admiration grew.

In the world of panhandling, this guy was a marketing maven. He understood the basics of fundraising: Tell them how much you need, how much you've taken in so far, where the money will go. Give prospective donors a sense of progress, of participating in a winning venture. By charting his intake, he would make even a modest handout seem urgent and valuable.

Not to mention that he was the only human standing outside on that bitter arctic night. By any standard, this was panhandling with a twist. Just why that twist hadn't turned into something more productive was anyone's guess.

I opened the window and handed him a dollar. He thanked me, I wished him luck, and the light changed.

❦

A woman I know owns a house on Cape Cod that she rents out for the summer. A large home in a desirable town, it rents for a hefty sum. When I asked recently if she'd had any problems with tenants, her answer fairly shrugged off the notion. In that price range, she implied, people are of a caliber that transcends trouble.

Among the illusions that guide people's thinking, that's a favorite with landlords. Others are equally trite—that a person's appearance is a metaphor for his housekeeping habits, and that timely payment of rent signifies something beyond itself.

As one who has owned a couple of rental condos in a nice suburb for many years, I can attest to the folly of these assumptions. Many of the old gauges of character that once led people into harmonious leasing arrangements no longer work. Which explains the conversation I had not long ago with a realtor.

Len called to say that he'd found new tenants, a young husband and wife, for my apartment. He'd left messages with their landlord and employers, in search of references. Of course, we could abridge all this, he said, if I chose simply to meet the couple, whom he described as lovely.

"They're all lovely," I quipped of tenants generically, "and they're still lovely when you meet them in court."

I explained that a meeting wouldn't tell me whether they could afford the rent, or how they cared for their home. That's where bosses and landlords fill in the gaps. Meeting one's tenants is a fine idea, albeit a dubious measure of creditworthiness or character.

Consider the case of Bob, a young policeman on the verge of marriage. In my conversations with him, Bob was even-handed, formal, and polite, a throwback to his days as a marine. Neighbors in the building found him friendly and considerate, an all-around good guy. The truth, however, was less flattering. The problems began as soon as he moved in: His first rent check bounced. When I subsequently refused to accept personal checks, money orders would arrive each month instead. Yet that, too, quickly fell apart. One month, rent came in the form of two money orders from separate banks, and still shy of the full amount. So began a downward spiral that led to repeated promises of specific payment on a specific date, followed by lesser payment on a later date.

When he moved out, Bob still owed more than $1,000, which went unpaid for months. Then a week or so before our court date, a bank check arrived. As my attorney surmised, no cop would want this episode trailing him on a permanent record.

Then there was my tenant Elena, a single working mom in her forties. For four years, her monthly rent checks arrived early, her handwriting a model of flowing script. In my contact with her, Elena was pleasant and courteous, if a bit fretful. True, her teenage sons had been a source of concern with their cell phones and cigarette smoking outside the building. Behaving like teenagers, however, appeared to be their gravest offense, which is generally not punishable.

When Elena told me that she had bought her own place, I asked my broker to visit the apartment.

"You pay me to tell you the truth," the broker said, "I have two words for you: dung heap."

Then came an inventory: dishes piled high in the sink; mildew in the bathroom; a broken window; two doors with holes the size of fists punched through them; a dented dishwasher that looked like it had been in a car wreck. By any reasonable standard, this was vandalism and neglect, pure and simple.

I can recite tales of other tenants who walked out on leases, damaged property, or otherwise displayed total indifference toward the contract or the place. And yet, if you asked their neighbors about these people, you'd be likely to hear praise. So much for politeness and early rent checks.

❧ ❧

America is a nation of voters. Of course, there are millions who aren't registered, and millions more who, for various reasons, don't vote. Perhaps they're tired of voting. They're sick of the unending array of nagging, stressful choices that are thrust upon us every day.

Vote, vote, vote—that's all we ever do. We vote in real elections, and fake ones—"If the presidential election were held today . . ." pollsters muse—and everything in between. From the moment we wake up to the moment we go to bed, it's a referendum on daily life.

Do we start with Corn Chex or yogurt? Wear a striped tie? Take the train to work? And that's just for openers.

No sooner does the day begin than we're forced to make yet more choices: low-carb, no fat, decaf, single-breasted, double-knit, high octane, low impact, right now! All that, mind you, before we even get to work.

If voting is, by definition, expressing an opinion or choice, then we're all perennial voters. Nor do we reserve our opinions for the purely personal. We'll happily cast our vote to elect a Survivor, Apprentice, or American Idol. If *Idol* is truly the most populist of the shows, its winners chosen by viewer votes, *Apprentice* is the least. Donald Trump is an electoral college of one, his vote the reason for the show's being.

There's no end to the litany of issues we're asked to opine about. Given this chronic taking of our collective pulse, you'd think we were well-versed in the business of voting. But apparently not. Somehow, for millions of Americans, there's a disconnect between the countless choices we make each day and the civic ones that arise every four years. Truth is, they're all part of the same continuum. Never mind whether the issue is double latte or Democrat. What matters is the availability of choices and our freedom to choose.

❧❧❧

It's said that everyone wants a wife. That's not a sexist remark so much as it is a fact. The traditional wife boasts a domestic résumé that is without peer. She's a whiz at multitasking, a superb team player, a manager of the highest order. With credentials like these, it's perfectly clear why everyone—male and female alike—would want a wife of their own.

Now I don't claim to be the universal matchmaker, but I may have found the wife for all of us. Never mind about her age, her looks, even her marital status. I've never actually met Karen. But we've talked on the phone, she's made promises, her word is good.

Karen came into my life recently when I called about my bottled water delivery. For years now, I've had gallons of it delivered every month. Just how many gallons, however, is always a question. My standing order has long been two cases. What shows up each month is anyone's guess. Consistency is not the company's strong suit.

True, I could have switched to another company ages ago. But the recurrent error has had its perks: lots of free spring water. At that price, I can afford to be annoyed.

Enter Karen.

When I called to report last month's delivery snafu, I asked Karen to please check my record. As she went back in the files, she found a pattern of errors that set her in motion.

"It couldn't be that hard to deliver the proper amount of water," she observed. And so you would think.

Karen had a plan. She would speak to the driver who handles my route and to the district manager. She would make a change in the database. We would begin a series of monthly talks.

"We're going to stay together on this, and we'll bond, and I'll take care of it," she announced.

I liked her vigor, even if the bonding seemed a bit much.

The next week rolled around and, sure enough, a message was waiting on my voice mail the morning of my delivery day. Just a reminder that Karen was on the case. That afternoon, my water wasn't just delivered. The boxes—two, to be exact—were stacked neatly like a little fortress by the door. The phone rang at five. It was Karen calling to confirm that all had gone as planned. I thanked her for a job well done and we agreed to talk in a month.

It may not be clear why Karen is my candidate for the universal wife. But the evidence should speak for itself: She sees a problem and solves it. She's dutiful, efficient—she gets the job done. While lesser talents at the firm have dabbled with my account for years, it was Karen who, in one fell swoop, eradicated the problem. In a more perfect world, Karen would be heading up some conglomerate, streamlining corporate waste. Instead she's found her niche in customer service, which is, arguably, the daily lot of the traditional wife. She listens to endless complaints and solves endless problems.

Frankly, I wish I could hire Karen to deal with my roof and wiring problems, and sundry other troubles that linger unresolved. I'm sure she'd whip things into shape in no time.

CHAPTER NINE: FAMILY AND FRIENDS

"I'm calling with condolences for your lost youth," I said, sarcas-
tically. "Happy Birthday!" And so went the message I left on
my friend's voice mail on the occasion of her fortieth.

Susan had a rough year. She had moved into a new house, a new
marriage (her third), and a new body, thanks to an extra, unwanted twenty pounds. The year also threw a curve ball: Susan was to
have an operation, which she put off as long as possible. When she
finally had the surgery, an unexpected tumor turned up—and it
wasn't benign. They had removed a cancer.

I remember Susan's phone call the day of the biopsy report.
The conversation was detailed, matter-of-fact. But the panic in her
voice was beyond anything I could hope to calm. More than anything, I just wanted to proclaim some soothing medical certainty
beyond my purview; all that was needed, though, was to affirm the
certainty of our friendship. This was too easy.

But I had no illusions. Though I had been in life-threatening
situations, I had never been diagnosed with an illness that could
be fatal. That was the line of demarcation. I didn't presume to
understand, in the pit of my being, how Susan felt. The best I
could hope for was to extend my own fear, to imagine how awful
this must be, and to hope that I was at least somewhere in the
ballpark. That is, perhaps, the nature of empathy—just being in
the ballpark.

As the months went by, talk of Susan's health lightened considerably. She would offer information about tests and doctors' visits
and treatments, thereby relieving my burden to ask. In a sense, she
became my tour guide; follow her lead, and the conversation would
go where she directed. I had only to trust that direction and desire
were the same. Presumably what we weren't discussing was not on
her itinerary.

But how could I know that for certain?

Perhaps she felt some subjects were too delicate, or weighty, or difficult to bring to the fore. Maybe she erased some destinations from her map so as to avoid adding them to mine; we're all so busy not burdening one another. Perhaps I should simply have asked: Is there more, or something else, or another way you'd like me to handle this?

While pondering, I couldn't help but think back to Susan's role when the tables were turned. When my mother was dying of cancer, Susan's daily phone call was like a shot of adrenaline. At times, she nearly revived me. Other times, I don't recall a word she said—I assume she must have been listening. Either way, our talks were always fortifying.

So I've wondered about the current situation, and my role in it, and whether or not I've really been in the ballpark. When I compare the two circumstances at hand, I recognize the errors in my equation: Susan was not dying, nor should friends necessarily mimic one another. If we can balance each other—where Susan offered energy, I provide steadiness—that makes for a truer mix. We don't reinvent ourselves for a crisis; we call upon what we are.

Susan called me back last night, right before midnight, before her birthday officially ended. She wanted to convey the results of her latest x-rays. Word is that everything is clean and negative, with no traces of danger. In a matter of weeks, her chemotherapy will end.

While birthday gifts and greetings were the order of the day, this news clearly took the cake. What other gift could even come close?

✥

Over the holidays, I received a box of fancy chocolate-covered strawberries. No ordinary fruits, these. As I opened the box, I ogled a dozen beauty queens, impossibly plump and tarted-up for the holiday season. I read the gift message and proceeded to dig in. First, I sampled one of the dark chocolate variety, which was bittersweet, rich, and smooth. The berry itself was respectable, too, until I reached the upper third. The bright red had soured into a pale green, unripeness spoiling the whole effect. A second strawberry was equally wan.

I thought of my friend, Emily, at the other end of the transaction, hoping to please with this decadent treat. Surely she hadn't meant to send a dazzling dud of a gift. Should I simply thank her for a clever, generous present, or share my critique, as well?

So began an inner debate on the ethics and etiquette of such a predicament: If you order from a company based on its stellar reputation, and the recipient politely thanks you for a defective gift, then the firm's reputation goes unchallenged, and you (mistakenly) think you've succeeded. The firm, perhaps unwittingly, continues to ship unripe berries, and buyers continue to purchase the product because no one bothered to tell the truth. A losing proposition all around. Indeed, I had planned to tell Emily of the problem, but only after it had been resolved.

First, I wanted to give the berry company, with its much-touted guarantee, a chance to rectify the situation. Two days later, a new box of chocolate-dipped strawberries arrived. Though the company had failed on the first go-round, its customer service excelled. Still, the second parcel was not without issues. A ruptured coolant pack had soaked every layer of cushioning down to, and including, the berries.

But that's a different story, for another time.

As luck would have it, Emily asked for an honest report on the product, claiming that she was doing research. She wanted to know if such outsized fruit could possibly have much flavor. I allowed that bigger is definitely not better in the world of strawberries, and that ripe is preferable to the unready product I received. I then thanked her for a terrific gift idea that proved more fruitful for discussion than eating.

᙭

My father was a complicated man—smart, thoughtful, and generous. Yet he was seemingly unfazed by his own racial prejudice. Like many people, he would say things in private that he knew he shouldn't. Among his targets of choice were African Americans.

When I was in high school, my father would utter racial epithets at dinner, knowing he'd get a rise out of my mother and me. My mother would roll her eyes and sigh. Other times, she'd turn a deaf ear and suggest I do the same. Just ignore his remarks and they'll go away. Sure enough, she was right. My dad's racial slurs declined in direct proportion to their audience.

I'll never know what motivated my father's prejudice, or what he really felt. I suspect that his views, like so much racism, were largely abstract: it wasn't that he disliked black people—he just didn't know many. But I remember when that changed and why.

It was the late 1960s when my father owned a small toy store. One day, a young black couple came in to do their Christmas shopping. My father struck up a conversation with the husband, Dan, an earnest, good-looking guy who was down on his luck. As I recall, Dan's job was on the line and one of his kids was in the hospital—it was a rough time all around. Dan left his phone number and said he'd be available for any odd jobs that might come up.

So began a twenty-five-year relationship that was choreographed around race.

Dan never knew what to call my father. "Mr. Silverman" sounded too stiff, and "Harold" too familiar, so he settled on "Boss." My father enjoyed the playful respect inherent in that nickname, and it set the terms between them.

Over the years, Dan worked for my father under various guises— as a maintenance man, mover, carpet cleaner, factotum. Nor did they have any fixed arrangement regarding payment. Dan would paint my dad's office, for instance, and the two of them would review the job after the fact. Then they'd agree on a fair price. The relationship relied on mutual trust.

All the while, my father and Dan bantered endlessly about race. They would joke about being black and white, respectively, noting their unmistakable differences. Bystanders, myself included, might blanch at the bald-faced remarks that amused these two grown men, but there was apparently some deeper process at work. By constantly referencing my father's whiteness, and Dan's blackness, they were navigating a racial minefield.

Eventually my father's racial slurs went by the boards. In their place he had a new mantra that he'd proudly declare. "I trust Dan like a son," he would say.

I don't know that the relationship between these two men ended my father's prejudice, but it certainly made a dent. As any observer could see, their odd friendship delighted them both.

꒰ꔫ꒱

There are two kinds of people in the world—those who embrace online networking, and those who don't. There's the Facebook-LinkedIn-Twitter set, on the one hand, who revel in all forms of digital connectivity, and the hold-outs, who aren't so sure.

Into the fray come my pals, Sharon and Jim. Yesterday they emailed a request to family and friends. Could we please keep their names off any and all social networks, blogs, and other online media?

Most notable was the benign nature of their complaint. There were no damaging facts, controversy, or scandal that they sought to expunge. Rather, it was the persistence of simple information, such as their home address, professions, even good-natured chatter about them, on the e-pages of people they barely knew, that so rankled them. In these Kardashian-crazed times, they didn't want even truthful tidbits of their lives being bandied about like so much gossip.

I re-read my friends' note and tried to grasp the sheer scope of the challenge. In an age when cookies track our every move on the web, and people volunteer all manner of data, Sharon and Jim merely want to be left alone.

"Yes, I know," Sharon says, "this is a futile attempt at a private life."

SOMEDAY THIS WILL FIT

Indeed. If they're serious about their goal, a plea to friends is hardly a solution. The Witness Protection Program would be a better bet.

Readers might well conclude that Sharon and Jim are probably Luddites, certainly misanthropes or loners. Not so. In fact, both of these middle-aged contrarians have worked at leading high-tech firms, and they use all the latest gadgets. Moreover, among those who know him, Jim is the go-to guy for technical and computer-related questions. Luddites, they're not.

Nor are they antisocial. They just prefer an old-school model of friendship that stems from first-hand encounters, where the bonds are more personal than virtual, and go beyond the electronic realm. For Sharon and Jim, it's obviously too late to "unfriend" the world that has landed unceremoniously on their digital doorstep. But their message is clear: even the most innocuous factoids may be more than some folks wish to share. Which is their right, however arcane or implausible. And it's equally the right of others to mention Sharon or Jim online in harmless, truthful ways, despite their wish for privacy.

In the end, Sharon and Jim's appeal may well be a cautionary tale for us all. As their friend, I'll gladly do my part to aid and abet their request, however pointless that may be. So, too, if everyone they know goes along with the program, the result will be the same. Alas, the privacy we've lost to the internet won't likely be reclaimed. As the Sharons and Jims of the world beg to be left out of the chatter, I envision the omnivorous PacMan, chomping his way through their plea.

※※※

Home gardeners are a notoriously competitive lot. They'll quietly wage war over matters of color, design, profusion of blooms—anything to outdo a neighbor's plot. When the neighbor is someone like my friend Judy, however, the exercise is all but pointless. Judy is the kind of gardener who, mid-career, upped and left a cushy, high-tech job to pursue a life with plants. She took up the study of landscape architecture, and went to work for a firm. Though her scheme didn't ultimately pan out, it wasn't for lack of talent. Her diverse, lovely garden sprawls around the side and back of her house, the envy of all who visit. It's a model of city gardening, a showcase of smart design.

One of the plants in Judy's garden is a lemon tree. Last summer it produced very few fruits, one of which was sitting on the kitchen counter one day—small and green, arguably unripe. That was indeed Judy's position: it had fallen off the tree by accident, and needed time to ripen.

I was not convinced. Looking at the fruit, I realized I had never seen a lemon like this, so perfectly round and small, clear-skinned, free of pock marks. This was no lemon, I declared—it was a lime.

And so began our year-long battle to claim the proper identity for this dubious citrus tree, whose sole job was now to produce for us. True, I had written magazine articles about horticulture, and I knew something about the subject. But I was no match for Judy in this arena. We were on her turf, in every sense, and I clearly recognized that fact. Still, I was sure this was a lime we were dealing with, and fifty dollars was now riding on it.

Proof of my foolishness came in a file box that first day, when Judy pulled out the name tag that had come with the plant. *Citrus limonia*, it said, without equivocation. It claimed to be a lemon tree. I argued that the plant was clearly mismarked, the wrong tag placed in its soil. And besides, since when is everything we read true?

Then there was the taste test. When I cut into the fruit, my conviction was only bolstered. Unlike the thick, fleshy rind of a lemon, this rind was evenly thin, more lime-like. Though the pulp was a pale, enervated green, it was green, nonetheless. The taste was that of a bitter lime. The details, it seemed, were mounting in my favor.

But Judy wouldn't budge. We needed a professional opinion. So we sent off some leaves to a local garden center for examination. When I phoned to get the verdict, the jury was still out: two staff horticulturists couldn't agree on the identity of the plant, so similar are the leaves of lemon and lime trees. The horticulturist told us to wait for the following spring and bring in the whole plant. Only then could a positive ID be made.

As we waited for the seasons to change, I took every opportunity to tease Judy on the subject. At one point, I was shopping at Crate & Barrel, when I happened upon a display of bright porcelain bowls. They were filled with assorted plastic fruits that were remarkably life-like. I negotiated with the cashier to buy one of these store props—a lemon that was a dead ringer for the real thing. I wrapped it in a white gift box and presented it to Judy.

For a few seconds there, she thought I was giving her an actual lemon.

In the perfect comeback, Judy drilled a tiny hole atop the fake fruit, and wired it to the tree. Alongside the occasional small green fruit was this full-grown specimen in shiny yellow. The joke had come full circle: Unwittingly, guests would admire the lemon for its hearty, good form. Meanwhile, limes were growing nearby on the same plant.

We never made it back to the garden center to confirm which type of citrus had incited our debate. Over time, unripe gave way to undeniable, and Judy finally gave in. A lime tree, it was.

In an ironic footnote, Judy told me last week that a common garden slug had taken up residence on the toy lemon. It had stationed itself on this plastic facsimile, as if it were an authentic fruit. As jokes go, this one was on us.

✤

Plagiarism is nasty business. Not only does it presume willful lifting of another's work; it suggests a larger taint on one's character. But what about plagiarism's kinder cousins? Adapting and deriving, for instance, are far-lesser crimes—if they're crimes at all. And what of the attribution that's simply unknown or plainly wrong?

Nowhere are these issues more clouded, absurd, or intriguing than in the kitchen. Take the case of my mother's Chocolate Angel Pie, a mousse-like concoction that sits in a billowing meringue shell. When I was growing up, that pie was linked with my mother. It was "her" pie. Not that she claimed its authorship, but she was its leading purveyor.

Actually, I think the recipe came from a package of Baker's Chocolate. But no matter: This is the stuff of which family legends are made, and who in the family would dare quibble? Besides, not everyone could master this delicate confection.

As time went on, the recipe filtered down to us. My brother and two cousins became the next generation of bakers, each working with the same instructions. Somehow, though, none of the pies turned out the same. My brother was the only one who accurately reproduced my mother's efforts. He got all of the highlights—taste (semisweet), texture (finely whipped), and color (deep taupe). My cousins, though excellent bakers, made great-tasting facsimiles that were decidedly wrong. One was too pale next to the hearty tone of the original; the other was flecked with chocolate bits, textured beyond the recipe's scope.

These are hardly criticisms of a pie that can't be ruined, but they illustrate an odd fact: Three attempts to quote an original source can lead to three distinct results. Despite the use of identical ingredients, and the same formulation, my cousins' pies were more paraphrase than quote—delicious approximations, not replicas.

Of course, my mother would have been pleased by all of these efforts, their intent so obviously flattering. If asked, she might even have coached the aspiring imitators. But in the annals of replication, only my brother has ever succeeded in baking a true copy. Our cousins are, alas, failures in the art of theft.

At some point, it seems odd to attribute three different pies to one recipe. Yet it was that one recipe that led three cooks down different paths. Whose pie is this, anyway?

In my view, it was my mother's pie by way of a recipe that she found. Chances are, she altered some detail or other, and the resulting pie was the one with her moniker. That's how many family

SOMEDAY THIS WILL FIT

recipes come into being—verbatim, with a little tweaking.

But given the real differences between the original pie and these failed wannabes, why shouldn't my cousins claim their versions to be their own? This would hardly be plagiarism; if anything, it would be a show of deference—an acknowledgement that not all Chocolate Angel Pies are created equal.

In the end, the origin of a pie is of little consequence, except for the matter of bragging rights. Within families, those rights escalate into stories, then legends, and the recipes become a shorthand between generations. It is unlike the commercial world, where a recipe might be one's trademark, and its theft the grounds for litigation.

Fortunately, most pies are made to be eaten, not chewed on by the law.

CHAPTER TEN: MOTHER LODE

In the normal course of events, daily life hums along until it doesn't. Something crops up and bumps things off course, ratcheting up the tenor of activity for a time. Then life resumes as usual, a reminder of the cyclical nature of things.

The ordinary and the extraordinary have always traveled in tandem, alternating in their own sort of alliance. It makes sense, for instance, that a major illness or accident makes everything else seem minor by comparison. Yet it's precisely at such times, when emotions tend toward the operatic, that people seek the common cadences of life. That's one of the lessons I learned from my mother, years ago, as she was dying.

We knew my mother's time was short—the doctors spoke in terms of months. Early on, while she could still go about the business of daily living, she was determined to do just that. She insisted on doing the laundry, for instance, which entailed numerous trips back and forth to the basement. Yet when I offered to help, she refused assistance. To her, laundry signified the comfort of familiar routines. That she could still cart the clothes and manage the stairs meant that she was still in the game.

And who were we to argue?

Then there was the matter of ice cream. One night my mother wanted peppermint stick ice cream from a particular shop, and I dared to propose an alternative. Selfishly, I was thinking of spending time together, not squandering it driving farther for a particular brand. In the end, my mother had her ice cream and ate it, too. Nor was her point lost: sometimes small incidentals trump loftier motives.

Or there was the afternoon a cousin came by to visit. My mother had been looking through a stack of mail when she happened upon a flyer from the supermarket. This, in turn, led to a conversation about the rising price of produce.

Later as my cousin was leaving, she remarked privately that she couldn't imagine how my mother, only weeks from death, could be interested in the cost of cantaloupe. I laughed and assured her that it was exactly the conversation my mother wanted. It was further proof that the engines of domestic life were in working order.

Today, looking back, I think about my mother's final months and her defiance about the ordinary details of living. True, a terminal illness changes the rules: a dying person, when able, calls the shots; the rest of us merely observe. The ordinary and the extraordinary mingle in ways that are, at times, surreal and hard to fathom.

In the end, I can recall thinking that my family was going through both the worst and most ordinary of human events. If it was in some way extraordinary, it was because my mother knew better.

✘✦✘

It was Mother's Day. We drove out to the cemetery, an hour away, to visit my grandmother's grave. It was a warm, sunny afternoon, at the height of spring. When we arrived, I reached into the back seat to take out the flowers, a dozen pale orange gladioli. We walked through several rows of weathered tombstones to the family plot. I leaned over and placed the flowers on my grandmother's grave. My mother then reached forward to adjust the stems slightly. The lake, a hundred yards away, was gleaming.

"Grampy always loved this lake," she said. "He thought it would be a peaceful place to go fishing."

Variations on this theme had been reenacted every Mother's Day for nearly forty years: my mother would buy flowers, go to the cemetery, visit her mother's grave. It was a ritual I'd never observed. Indeed, I had never been to the cemetery before, never seen the family plot. My presence on that day was as an accomplice. My mother was too sick to drive and it was important that she go. She was terminally ill and this would be her last visit with her mother. So I drove to the cemetery for the first time, knowing that I would be back soon for a different occasion.

Frankly, my mother had no business making the trip at all. She slept both ways in the car and was barely strong enough to walk when we got there. To her failing body, the simple, flat terrain of the cemetery was more like a mountain. But she insisted upon going, nonetheless. Good sense, at times, is merely an insult.

When I laid the flowers on my grandmother's grave, I remember not wanting to be there. I had come as transportation, and now I felt like an intruder. My mother leaning forward to rearrange the flowers only confirmed this. Bending over was so impossibly difficult for her at this stage—and yet, the flowers apparently had to be moved. Only she could move them. I knew instantly that this revision was not aimed at me. It was the final gesture of a daughter saying goodbye to her mother.

In fact, I wasn't an intruder at all that day, but a bystander witnessing a ritual that started before I was born. It was my mother's way of being a daughter—to bend when there was no bending left, that the flowers would lie just so against the stone.

⚜

"You know, parents aren't supposed to live forever," she said.

That was how my mother broke the news, seven years ago, that she was dying of cancer. She then spent the next three months composing the death she wanted—a death that would affirm the life she had lived and the way she would be remembered.

My mother was only half-right. Parents do live forever. Some just do it better than others.

For weeks during her illness, my mother put on a great performance. Every day she would muster energy that she no longer had, reciting lines that were no longer true, in order to bolster a fantasy.

It's hard to know whose fantasy it was anymore. Was it ours, or hers? Were we in collusion?

My brother, who lived in Texas at the time, would call every afternoon. For five or ten minutes each day, he would hear the reconstituted mother-voice—that ultimate shield with its lifetime of mothering behind it. It was the voice that comforted and reassured, that could convince a child that everything would be alright.

Nor was this just for my brother. One effect of the phone ritual, every day for ten minutes, was the coup of convincing herself as well. The daily theater piece was self-resuscitating: it was how my mother breathed life into herself. But as time went on, the actress and the role grew farther apart and the theater became more absurd. Would I go along with my mother, saying nothing, and engage in a sort of collective fraud? Or would I tell my brother, half a continent away, that what he heard on the phone was no longer strictly true?

I did both.

"She does this for you and for herself," I would explain. "But she's really not doing very well."

I would then detail some of the decline if my brother was about to come east to visit. At close range, it seemed the truth had a purpose. But at a distance, on the phone and with no visit pending, what was the point? After all, it was no secret that she was dying.

Today I spoke with my friend Emily, whose mother is dying the same motherly death. She is reciting the lines she wants to say, wants to hear, wants her children, however grownup, to believe. It was fine when Emily was in New York with her mother, hearing her mother's rendition of the truth with its carefully constructed edges. But now that Emily is back home in L. A., it's different.

"How's your mother doing?" I ask.

"I don't really know," she says, explaining that, in spite of the near-daily phone calls, there is always the mother factor. That's the difference between what is said and what is meant, between what's medically true and what's fundamentally true about these women.

"Do you have any reliable source of information?" I ask.

"Not really," she says. "I struggle to understand."

Let them have their evasions and lies, their old-world courtesies. That our mothers refuse to suffer loudly is as much a matter of luck as of manners and mettle. Dying doesn't always permit such options.

But for some mothers, whose love protects and guides and is unravaged by the disease that takes them, it is a wish fulfilled—to orchestrate a death in concert with the life they lived.

❧

The invitation arrived in the mail. It would be a fancy affair, requiring more civilized garb than I usually wear. I go to the closet and stare into a sea of jerseys, blouses, slacks—the mainstays of my daily life. Nowhere in front of me is there a proper dress or suit. Such costumes are located to the right of center, in the more conservative recesses of the closet. There I begin the search for what I know to be buried inside. For this is a story about coming out of the closet—about a wardrobe lost and found, unearthed and born again.

One by one, to the deep right, I exhume heavy-laden hangers covered in suit bags, their contents a mystery to me. I lift up the coverings to reveal a double-breasted gray suit, then a navy wool suit, then skirts and tops, and finally, a dress in basic black.

I place my body inside their various forms, mindful that I am trying on a range of different selves. There are the obvious disparities of tone—the business suit, the evening dress, the casual skirt. Then there are the discords of scale—larger and smaller versions of myself, none of which gets abandoned when another takes hold. Life is short—and so, often, is weight loss. Then there are the variations of age and style. Conservative taste keeps me squarely in an eternal fashion warp—"in" or "out" are merely states of mind.

But the true measure of a closet is in the richness of its memories, the associations that it evokes.

I remove the bag that conceals the black dress. I remember buying it eight years ago and trying it on for my mother. Without a word being said, she knew absolutely why I had gotten it.

She was dying; it was no secret. I bought the dress for her funeral. I remember wondering whether to show it to her at all, debating whether it was just too morbid. Yet I knew how much she would love the dress, and me in it. And she did.

I also recall having bought the dress with the full knowledge that I would probably wear it only once. I assumed it might be difficult to wear again, made grim by the events that occasioned its purchase. But eight years later, I stand looking in the mirror, surprised. There is, alas, more of me in that dress now, though all of me is happier to be there.

And I was wrong: it was not the dress that was grim, just the circumstances. I would gladly wear it again.

A closet, it might be argued, is a darkroom for the psyche, a place where pictures of oneself get developed. Front and center, for those who arrange their closet by traffic patterns, is what one sees in the mirror each day. But it is the sidelines, the nooks and crannies, that hold deeper interest. There lie the selves one sees less often—the black dresses, the particular shoes. Therein lies the fuller tapestry of who we are.

⚘

The sun fell in stripes on the grass at the cemetery where we stood, a sea of navy suits. I was visiting for the first time in years. It's true that I wasn't visiting, exactly; we were attending a family funeral. But I was there on that grim day, made less grim by my mother's presence, buried nearby.

It was six years since I last visited, despite my fondness for this place. Not that I hadn't thought to visit many times before; but I've never been sure, exactly, of what's here. This rectangle in stone, over a wooden box, with whatever's left of flesh and bone—that's what I know is here. Beyond that, I am not at all certain.

I am certain, however, that my mother is still around. Last week, for instance, she showed up in a dream. We were sitting in the living room of the house where I grew up, the two of us talking. It felt like the most natural thing in the world, but for the subject: we were discussing my mother's funeral of seven years ago. I was explaining why we had waited two days between her death and the service—that various relatives were flying in from around the country. She listened eagerly, curious to know more. The conversation was spirited, familiar, as if in the present. My mother had aged several years; she looked and sounded just as I would have imagined.

When I woke up, I was so delighted by the dream, by having seen and spoken to her, that what we said barely even registered. I had captured her so credibly, so fully animated a still life, that I was tickled. For a few minutes, at least, my mother was alive.

"And by the way," she said as the dream was closing, "I've still got those letters. I read them from time to time; they sound so much like you." And with that, the dream ended.

Not to quibble, but I'm the one who has the letters. They were written in the final weeks of my mother's life, when I was racing against time.

During the three months of her illness, I visited my mother every day. I made lists of things to discuss with her—unresolved themes, lifelong disagreements, assorted loose ends. For weeks, I carried around this changing agenda, waiting for the right moments to broach one thing or another. Too often, though, I would leave the house at night, frantic that time was running out. With each passing day, my visits coincided less and less with her periods of clarity and alertness.

So I started writing letters that I would leave for her at night on the breakfast table.

Those letters were a turning point. I would read my words, and look at the list I carried around, only to find a hundred variations on one theme: Did she know absolutely that I loved her? It was perfectly clear that nothing else mattered. It was the one true thing, the only thing worth saying, or repeating, or demonstrating, or finding a way to make understood. The rest was details.

In truth, of course, my mother had known this all along; my business was not with her, but with myself. I threw out my lists a week or so before she died, and all of the fight and frenzy in me just fell away.

Seven years later, the sun falls in stripes on the grass at the cemetery. This morning, I am one of the navy suits, bearing witness. My mother, too, bears witness from her own vantage point: rectangle in stone, wooden box, her presence wherever it may be.

CHAPTER ELEVEN: SHOPPING

"Clerk to produce," the overhead voice blares. "Clerk to produce." Suddenly my trance is broken. I am wheeling my cart down the mustard aisle at my local supermarket, humming along with the background music. The music is not canned at all. It's real music, sung by the original artists, in a long, intoxicating loop. So smart is the compilation that I often dawdle just to hear the end of the current song.

Like many of the shoppers around me, I am fully immersed in the music. I have stashed my grocery list in my pocket; the music has freed me to improvise in each aisle. Stripped of my list, calmed by the tuneful haze, I am a blank check waiting to be written. Which raises some interesting questions.

It's often said that hit songs become certifiable classics when they're heard on elevators. But the same songs are played each day as part of a larger seduction, alongside the tofu. The psychology is clear: the hook is invariably love songs—songs filled with pining and longing and wistfulness. Up the ante with a heavy dose of vintage duets ("Up Where We Belong," "Feel Like Making Love"), and it's a perfect recipe for consuming.

Unlike the songs themselves, there is a sense of fully requited love: As shoppers, we jauntily hum and tap our way down the aisles, distractedly going about an otherwise drab routine. Presumably we also toss more products into the cart, only half-knowingly. We're pleased with the shopping encounter; the management is thrilled with the music system.

Exactly how all of this works is less apparent. As I approach the cookie aisle, for instance, Steve Perry is singing, pleading to my foolish heart. Do I then subliminally reach for the Oreos? Or do I consciously resist, plagued by images of padded hips and a loveless future?

More to the point, if Oreos weren't part of the plan in the first place, can Steve Perry pry open my heart so that I now must buy them?

I'm sure it happens. The music is mesmerizing; hum along with it, and the grocery tab is sure to rise. So it is a complex set of factors at work here, tempting us in one aisle, soothing us in the next. I'd like to claim that I'm above it all, unmoved by the Steve Perrys, the Stings, and the rest. In fact, I'm not. But my real vulnerability is of a different sort. Last week when I left the supermarket, I immediately updated the playlist on my iPhone.

Steve Perry now pleads to me directly, in the privacy of my own home.

❧ ❧

I was placing an order for some shirts. The saleswoman on the phone explained that, though the fall catalog wasn't out yet, new colors were in stock. "Blue Pine" and "Deep Sapphire" sounded intriguing. I pictured the medium blue-green of a forest and the cool, rich blue of the stone.

Lacking any photos or text, the saleswoman and I were left to speculate. We agreed that the colors should approximate their names—a circular approach, at best. With that, I placed my order knowing that I could keep, or return, the merchandise.

One might reasonably ask why so many souped-up shades and hues compete for our catalog dollars. One popular clothier lists more than sixty variations of blue in its current catalog, while another flaunts over seventy. These include aquatic blues (lagoon, lake, saltwater), earthier tones (chalk and stone), seafaring blues (admiral, mariner), and florals (indigo, iris, cornflower). Other blues claim, remarkably, to be "fresh" or "clear," while additives like "pale," "washed," and "heather" extend the palette.

Are so many nuances strictly necessary, or do they add some cachet or perceived value that eludes more basic nomenclature? After all, invoking subtle gradations of the ocean—surf blue, tidal blue, bay blue—conveys more in the way of mood than meaning.

Then there's the issue of common terminology. If two companies use the term "Atlantic blue," do they always mean the same thing?

In a word: no.

Even the audacious "true blue," which turns up in several catalogs, is agnostic. It may be bright or medium blue, depending on who's doing the naming. Color is in the eye of the copywriter.

Back to Deep Sapphire and Blue Pine. When the box arrived with my shirts, a dose of reality set in. There was neither stone nor forest—just two shirts in pleasing, if less poetic, shades of blue.

Should Blue Pine and Deep Sapphire, then, be dropped from the lexicon of shirt colors? Granted, they offer sparse guidance when it comes to describing shirts. Yet such names serve as vessels to be filled with one's own imaginings. In the end, whatever these names may lack in usefulness, they gain in sheer aura.

❧ ❧

Some people are bargain hunters. They set out for the mall in search of savings. I, on the other hand, am a bargain magnet. Not that I go looking for discounts—they simply find me.

Last week, I went shopping for a copier machine. Weighing the merits of various models, I asked the salesman some questions. He then pointed to a newer version of the Canon copier we had been discussing and I asked the price. Since it had just arrived that day, it was still unmarked. He excused himself and retreated behind the counter, where he scanned the product code on the box.

"It's forty dollars," he announced.

I laughed, as if to go along with the joke. When he didn't respond with a more plausible number, I challenged the price. Forty dollars would barely cover the cost of packaging and shipping, I argued, much less the product.

"You can't argue with the computer," he said, as if a machine were the final authority on pricing.

The forty-dollar copier went through yet another screening at the checkout counter, with the store's manager looking on. That was several layers of missed opportunity before the copier and I left the store.

Once home, I immediately checked the store's latest catalog, which had arrived recently in the mail. I looked up the copier model, and there it was in bold print: $199.99.

I suppose I could have picked up the phone, called the store manager, and restarted the debate. But I had already done battle once in person and had tired of the fight. Where does one's moral duty end and the store's responsibility begin?

Perhaps if unquestioning, robotic salespeople weren't the rule in so many stores, money wouldn't trickle out the door. I know, I know: most people would revel in such savings. I, on the other hand, am troubled by the frequency of these misplaced bargains.

Take, for instance, another shopping experience I had recently. A well-known home furnishings store had just received a shipment of Persian rugs. As I browsed the store, a lovely Hamadan caught my eye. Equally eye-catching was the price tag. Looking at similar Hamadans in the pile, I noticed that all of them were marked two, even three, times higher. Having bought several rugs before, I knew this was a steal. I just happened to be the thief who bought it.

Actually, I thought to question the price, but for two facts. The lone salesman in the department had told me that he was new and untrained. This didn't bode well. Moreover, the rugs were all one-of-a-kind. Unlike mass-produced goods that are identical in character and price, comparisons among hand-woven rugs are, at best, approximate.

In the end, I decided to leave well enough alone. Had the salesman agreed that the rug was mismarked, what then? Would he have refused to sell it to me? There was no one else in the department to ask, nor was the computer much help. And so I bought the rug for a song.

❧

I just solved all my problems. Well, not all of them, perhaps, but the ones that can be relegated to baskets, boxes, and trays. Unlike those who thrive on clutter, I find that a modicum of order goes a long way.

Call me a clutter-phobe. Too many piles of unassigned stuff give me the jitters, as if nothing will get done until the piles recede. That, of course, only feeds on itself, since there's no end to the oddments of daily life that need to be organized: a pile of catalogs here, a stack of papers there, stuff wedged under benches, in corners, at the edge of the desk—and all of it taking up valuable real estate.

Granted, neatness offers hope for redemption. But even neatness pales next to containment. Assorted bills and notices, newspaper clippings, a memo to tune the piano and clean the chimney—all can be neatly arranged and well-placed. Yet for some of us, the mere presence of this stuff is enough to activate some primal impulse. No, it's not an urge to tidy all forms of life; it is, however, a need to banish the more niggling stacks and piles, and to simplify the art of finding things.

Among the roads that lead to Mecca is the simple path I've taken. I recently went to one of those stores that sells the components to organize one's life. I roamed the endless aisles, awed by the breadth of possible ways to regulate and subdivide one's stuff. I looked at shelves (single, double, free-standing, wall-mounted, and modular); storage bins, book racks, and shoe holders; binders in leather, vinyl, and paperboard. In short, there were containers of virtually every description, size, and shape. Yet I was undaunted by so many prospects, cheered on by their very existence.

I confess that my first trip to the store was not your standard retail foray. It was more like visiting a museum, church, and therapist, all in one. I reveled in the artfulness of designs that proclaimed the notion that storage can be beautiful. The conventional box had been turned on its head, recast as object, texture, and color—and, yes, as a place to store things. Surrounded by the promise of whipping my material life into order (or at least into boxes), I found new clarity.

Clutter is an insidious thing, making its way from your desk to your "to do" list, and finally lodging in the brain. If Confucius didn't say this, surely he meant to: To unclutter the mind, first get yourself some boxes.

⁂

'Tis the season to annoy the people we love. Not that this is deliberate, mind you. It's part of the seasonal sport known as holiday shopping. Herewith, some common grievances.

"You're impossible" or "hard to please" are among the epithets widely heard at this time of year. On behalf of those implicated, I'm often amused by the stubbornness of our accusers. I gladly provide hints and clues to those who ask. I'm forever searching for the best strawberry jam and Medjool dates.

But how often do our critics come through with the very thing they begged to know?

Approximately never.

Do people really want gift ideas, or does such intervention undermine their wish to surprise and impress? I'd say the latter. The perfect gift isn't necessarily the thing you want; it's the thing you didn't know you wanted, which requires both stealth and cleverness on the part of the giver.

"Slippers," the message proclaimed on my voice mail. It was a friend announcing her discovery of the ultimate comfy footwear, which she was giving her sister for Christmas. Perhaps I, too, might like a pair?

I quickly responded, defending my favorite moccasins and thanking her nonetheless.

"Dear Foiler/Spoiler," she replied, exasperated, "You're just the sort of person I send moose lawn ornaments to!"

Then last week, another friend suggested that we modify our holiday exchange of gifts.

"Malawi," she proposed as an alternative. She asked that I make a donation, if I were so inclined, to feed people in Malawi.

At first, I bristled at the idea. A charitable donation is lovely, to be sure. But aren't there charities closer to home that urgently need our dollars?

Of course, I came around. My friend's idea made perfect sense, summoning us to less greed.

That I ultimately nixed it, however, reflected something else. I had already bought her gift and, separately, chose to donate to Katrina victims.

Which gets to the heart of the matter. Gifts can be an expression of many things—thanks, whimsy, thoughtfulness, élan. While suggestions may help, they can also thwart the giver's need to find, make, or choose something of one's own devising. This may be a point of pride, a show of insight, or a gesture of solidarity. Suffice it to say, gifts often function on multiple levels, many with subtext.

So, how to negotiate the thickets of gift giving this season?

Listen closely to talk of slippers and charity. Consider dates and jam. Then do what gift givers have done for years—namely, whatever you please.

※ ※ ※

I recently bought a new car. Like many latter-day car shoppers, I did much of my research online. These days, the internet has become a car buyer's point-of-entry. Consumers can arm themselves with an arsenal of information to prepare for the battle ahead.

Before setting foot in a showroom, I filled out a simple questionnaire at two manufacturers' websites and checked off the car models I was considering. In so doing, I was inviting local dealers to pitch their wares.

And pitch they did.

First came the promise, from one dealer, of the vehicle I wanted, at a cost that would be "agreeable" to me. He offered the identical car that I had priced on the manufacturer's website, only the price tag had changed—and not for the better.

Then came a second dealer with a different approach. This one sent an introductory email, then a few follow-ups. When I didn't respond, the emails stopped. The one-sided proceedings began and ended, appropriately, in the span of three weeks.

My favorite of the car correspondents, however, was a woman I'll call Linda. A "client care specialist" for a major dealership, Linda began with a "welcome" note, followed by a "thank you," then repeated reminders that I had, after all, requested information. When, after several days, I still hadn't replied, her sixth message began, "Did you get my last email?"

Frankly, Linda's emails not only went unanswered; they went unread. I had started looking at other makes of cars and was paying little attention to the posts gathering in my in-box. It wasn't until I saw a virtual stockpile of missives from her that I began to take note. They ranged from the informative (whether to buy or lease) to the inquisitive (are you still looking for a new car?), from the helpful (insurance tips) to the persistent (we "will not lose a customer over price," she wrote). One message included no less than four links that I could click to indicate my current status as a car buyer, with as many opportunities to curtail Linda's resolve.

Then came the Mother of All Headlines: "You never call. You never write."

This latest ploy would have amused me at any stage. But as the twenty-second message (literally) in Linda's ongoing sales blitz, arriving in the third month of this unrequited courtship, I had to roll my eyes. If timing is everything, then Linda's otherwise clever move was off by at least a month.

Linda and her counterparts are doubtless carrying on their sales tactics, alternately informing, amusing, and spamming would-be car buyers. Although I ended up buying a different make of car, Linda was hardly to blame. If anything, she only added to my respect for the low-key dealer who closed the sale.

❧❧

As thirty-three miners emerged from their underground ordeal in Chile several years ago, the world watched. This was the ultimate rescue: half a mile down, through solid rock, to the waiting men. For most of us, it was one of those leveling events. To paraphrase one television sportscaster, it was utterly bizarre to segue from the live satellite feed in Chile to the nightly sports recap while the first miners were surfacing, making history. Yet, life goes on, in all of its mundane glory.

By the next day, as the number of rescued miners continued to grow, I went about my business, which included a trip to the supermarket.

Most of us have some item or other on our grocery list that's either hard to find, or hard to find in quantity. So, when we find it, we do the obvious thing: wipe the shelves clean, thereby solving our own problem, and creating the same annoyance for others.

You got a problem with that?

So I'll buy all four boxes of my favorite crackers, for instance, or the last three jars of peach jam. It's a first-come, first-served marketplace, and there I am. If there's some reason to modify my purchase, it eludes me. Delaying now will only mean searching for more, later.

Recently, though, I've had a change of heart. Last week, there were six pints of my favorite cottage cheese in the refrigerated case, and I bought only five. Though I wanted the entire stash, I decided to leave one for the next frustrated shopper, as a token of solidarity.

By any reasonable standard, this was a tepid rendition of the golden rule. I make no claim to generosity—only a slight bow to courtesy. And since a decision to buy, or not buy, gives me no leg up on the ladder to sainthood, I dismiss the prospect of forfeiting all six pints.

There's charity, on the one hand—foolishness, on the other.

A second option might have been to split the remaining inventory with some imaginary shopper who had yet to materialize. Three pints for her, and three for me, would certainly be equitable. But then, I was there for the cottage cheese—and she wasn't.

As I wheeled my cart to the next aisle, I was thinking about the odd calculation I'd just made. There's no right answer to this little quandary. People will arrive at their own number, and for their own reasons. Of course, I hope the karma of cottage cheese may turn up later—that one pint left behind now will be another that awaits me in the future.

Then I thought back to those Chilean miners, with their teaspoon of tuna fish and their desperately scant supplies. At that moment, I understood exactly how the sportscaster felt chronicling the day's punts and tackles.

CHAPTER TWELVE: SAY, WHAT?

This is the week, between Christmas and New Year's, when the annual "Dear Friends" letters, those personal year-end reports, start to arrive. One of the better examples showed up in today's mail. It came from my friend Tom, who manages, in a single page, to survey the global landscape: he covers his wife and kids; Hillary Clinton and Donald Trump; Putin, ISIS, and the California draught.

"As you can see," he reassures us, "I have retained my bad attitude."

Compare this to the annual screed I receive from a woman named Jan. She devotes a full paragraph to each family member, citing awards and achievements, as if the entire family were job-hunting. Her letters are worse than precious; they affect just the right blend of wistfulness, candor, and well-being.

I'll admit that some of us view the arrival of these annual missives as a sporting event. We compare notes, wager on the various contenders (which is the most outrageous, the most amusing?), and otherwise share these deliberately public communiqués. We're exempt from the usual privacy constraints by virtue of the opening line: "Dear Friends" is an invitation to "Show-and-Tell"—and show and tell we do.

But what is it that comes over people when they engage in this yearly ritual?

Too often, the rules of social discourse are dropped in favor of some imagined higher laws of writing. Plain-speaking is out; inflated prose is in. The effect is, these letters often read like bloated résumés.

Whether one prefers such correspondence to be newsy, reflective, or wry, there is an art to the "Dear Friends" letter, as well as a few tricks. The art comes from the challenge inherent in any act of self-display. An annual letter attempts, above all, to convey the flavor and texture of the last year. It's a first-person chronicle that carries with it the danger of appearing self-absorbed.

How easily a simple description can become excessive—and suddenly you're showing a home movie to an audience of one.

The question of audience is, or should be, a real factor. I've often wondered if certain annual letters were meant for one set of readers, and the mailing list just grew. I'm not sure, for instance, that I need to know that my friend's son, Todd, has mastered potty training. That kind of news is best shared with family, if at all.

Furthermore, I've seen evidence that even the worst of years, given a clever spin, can make for great reading.

A friend, not long ago, had such a year, and still found a way to conquer the yearly letter: She mentioned briefly a death in the family, that her husband had lost his job, and that they had been forced to relocate out of state. But she spent most of the letter observing that the apple tree in their new yard had proved surprisingly prolific; that the cats were adjusting well to their new home; and that the forced move had taken on the air of an adventure.

My friend had taken a series of bad endings and recast them in the most hopeful light. It seemed like a triumph of both spirit and letter writing.

So the annual "Dear Friends" letters are being polished and mailed this week, as people close the book on another year. As with most things, it's rarely the content of these letters that makes them memorable. More often, it's their tone or point of view.

Of course, an empty envelope would speak volumes.

❧❧

Once again, it's that time of year when gifts abound and thank-you notes must follow.

While some people avert this issue by conveying their gratitude via phone, others face a thoroughly modern dilemma: whether to write, or email, their thanks. There are several schools of thought on this. Traditionalists argue that a hand-chosen gift warrants a handwritten note–period. Implicit is a kind of quid pro quo, and a sense of insult if the code is broken. Realists, by contrast, may also prefer handwritten notes but, sadly, have given up expecting, or writing, them. Then there are the modernists, who don't see what all the fuss is about. A thank-you note is a thank-you note, however it gets there.

Over distance and time, most of us can agree that the point of these notes has remained unchanged: to acknowledge the thoughtfulness of someone's gesture. For gifts that arrive by mail, a "thank you" also confirms that the gift actually arrived. In the digital age, however, finding a suitable middle ground isn't so simple. The fact is, most of our online life conveys an air of speed and impulse, not of care and thought. Emails are typically dashed off, as if they're postscripts. The medium doesn't encourage composition or revision, the slow processes of hammering ideas into words. So, even when an email is carefully written, it comes with a certain taint. No amount of deliberation or artful editing can override that guilt by association.

So there it is. You can spend the same amount of time tapping out an electronic thank-you–shaping, refining, reworking the prose–as you would a handwritten letter. Click "send," and it arrives instantly, without fanfare, alongside assorted coupons, renewal notices, and other spam. By contrast, had you handwritten the same note, and pasted a postage stamp on the envelope, it would probably be welcomed as an oasis in a sea of bills. Which, by the way, is one of the more elemental reasons we should care about the survival of snail mail. Without it, we'd never know what anyone's handwriting looked like anymore.

Still, there's a strategy for those who want their digital words to earn the same cred as those written on paper. Amid the plethora of error-laden, unpunctuated, lowercase emails that fill most of our in-boxes, well-crafted exceptions will always stand out.

Like a shirt that's neatly pressed, even a thank-you note benefits from a little grooming.

❧

I was paying bills one afternoon, writing checks. Then it dawned on me why the date I kept writing over and over looked oddly familiar. I picked up the phone to call Molly and wish her a happy birthday.

"How did you remember?" she asked.

"Some things you just don't forget," I said.

We spent an hour or so catching up and trading news, filling in the gaps. We weren't in much contact these days and hadn't been since a falling out ten years before. There was no fight, or even a disagreement between us—it was one of those misunderstandings that just took on a life of its own. Except for a few notes exchanged by mail when there was a death in each of our families, we didn't speak for six years.

It's not uncommon that friends lose touch for extended periods: kids arrive on the scene, a new job requires travel, a divorce complicates everything. But a long, strained silence between friends has its own architecture. It forms a foundation, then walls, then structural supports that are self-sufficient. Over time, the silence becomes a fortress through which there's no entry.

Molly and I had built such a fortress purely by staying out of touch. So when I sent her a note, six years later, my point was not to rebuild the friendship; it was to start the demolition process.

At first we spoke nervously, then candidly, and managed to clear a path. But how could we figure out what happened six years before, when it was never really clear at the time?

We couldn't.

Instead we relied on the good faith of an old friendship that had stumbled on some unexpected fault line. A few days after we spoke, I received an invitation to a family party Molly was throwing. Handwritten on the front were the words, "You're always welcome." In the scheme of things, her words seemed more wishful than true. But if normalcy was not yet possible, graciousness was a fine stand-in.

Over the next few years, Molly and I spoke and visited on several occasions. While the visits became warmer with time, the simple ease of our early friendship was never really restored. I always sensed that our miscue had left some residual doubt. So I was glad when, on her birthday, the conversation had a different tone.

I'll never really know what caused the tangle with Molly, or why it spiraled into something else and hardened into years of silence. Nor am I sure where we are right now on the spectrum of friendship—whether we're at some fixed point at a safe distance, or moving in some clear direction.

Meanwhile, Molly and I continue to chat on occasion, our newsy, catch-up talks an easy medium. The sturdy friendship we had in the past is gone. Only time will tell whether two old friends, still fond of each other, will build on the loss.

❧

When my neighbor's mother died recently, I sent a donation to charity in her name. The following week, my neighbor sent an engraved card, thanking me for my "kind expression of sympathy."

Inside a handwritten note reiterated the sentiment. "I really appreciate your thoughtfulness," it might have said. But, no, it was my "thoughtfulness!"—with an exclamation point—that she appreciated. Indeed, three of the four sentences in her note ended with that graphic mark of surprise.

Was my "thoughtfulness!" so completely unexpected?

Or perhaps "thoughtfulness," left to itself, unadorned, seemed too sober or candid.

It's hard to know what prompts such grammatical excess in otherwise reasonable adults. But I'd be willing to bet that it stems from an earlier phase of life.

Face it. Unlike other forms of punctuation, the exclamation point is decidedly feminine–girlish, even. By that, I don't mean the occasional solitary use of the basic stick-and-dot design.

I'm referring to multiple exclamations of the bulbous style used by teenage girls. When this icon appears, it shows up in spades. Every idea is exclamatory! Every thought, a revelation!

Perhaps we should simply accept that the exclamation point was long ago appropriated by teenagers. They are, after all, its chief proponents. It suits the drama of adolescent life, with its flouting of boundaries and rules. So when it turns up in adult writing on more than an occasional basis, it seems like a leftover–a throwback to the giggly excess of earlier years.

I don't know how punctuation is taught these days in school, or whether the exclamation comes with suitable disclaimers: Like bay leaves and dill, the exclamation point should be used sparingly. Otherwise it spoils the flavor of the surrounding text. When everything is a surprise!, a revelation!, then nothing surprises. It all tastes the same.

Back to the thank-you note from my bereaved neighbor. Truth is, my neighbor is girlish in the extreme. As a teenager, she doubtless reveled in every opportunity to dot her "i's" with a bubble, and end her sentences with numerous and shapely exclamation points. On balance, then, her now simpler stick-and-dot style, though still excessive, has grown up and pared down.

☙❧

I used to worry about small envelopes finding their way through the mail. It seemed amazing that millions of standard business envelopes arrived at their destination each day, without a hitch. A modest notecard, by contrast, stood to get buried or lost in the crush. It's rough out there in the postal world, landing in boxes, baskets, and trucks, amid rivals with far more clout.

Then came the little envelope that could. First off was its color—a deep assertive red that was more statement than hue, easily grabbing the eye. And it was translucent, leaving no hint of mystery about its contents. I could just picture it whizzing by countless bigger and blander envelopes without apology. Getting lost was not an option. Inside was a green-and-red notecard with a diamond-in-circle pattern, reminiscent of a man's necktie. So dense was the overall effect that no writing would have been legible on the envelope's face; a separate mailing label was needed.

"Do you think this card is a little on the bright side?" my friend wrote. "The red of the envelope is the same red as the pajamas my husband got me that I refused to wear to bed because they kept me awake. I'm surprised he could sleep through all the red noise."

Granted, many people would don those pajamas, turn off the light, and have done with it. Minutes later, they'd be sound asleep. Others, like my friend, however, would toss and turn in the knowledge that they resembled a fire engine, tucked in bed. They'd worry about the sheets and whether the adjacent colors might clash, thereby ruining their prospects for rest. While such concerns may not be common to everyone, many of us can relate.

Waking up in a Santa Claus suit, for instance, could well startle the morning-impaired. Frankly, for some of us, even the thought of a bold color seems antithetical to the notion of sleep.

❧ ❧

When Carol died not long ago, we had known each other for about fifteen years. We weren't close or good friends, but we were some form of friends, casually, over many years. I could never have defined it, exactly; there were so many shifts, over time, from a business relationship to a more social one. So, when Carol's husband called, two days after she died unexpectedly, I was surprised almost as much by the timing and tone of his call as by the fact of her death.

Greg apologized, in earnest, for not having called sooner—*sooner?*—and somehow answered questions I had never asked. Here was a woman with countless friends and acquaintances; who sat on every committee, charity, and board; who had a family, ran a business, and traveled constantly. And yet, here I was, receiving this phone call, not a month, or a week, after she died—but two days later, and with apology.

Could I have been wrong about the friendship? Had I underestimated it?

Sometimes it's perfectly clear what a friendship is, or isn't; it needs no defining. When I talk to my old friend Annie, there's nearly a silence that surrounds my words. That's her way of listening, almost audibly, as if to hear so closely will dissolve any possible barrier. I have never encountered anything quite like it. There's no cutting to the chase, or rush—just this listening that gently urges, through silence, to the heart of things.

The friendship with Annie contains so much code and chemistry, it requires virtually no work. It is a model, in one sense, of how friendships evolve over time. Still, I remarked recently to a friend, "You know, it's funny. I'm closer to Annie, but I love you more."

Joyce looked at me quizzically, shaking her head, and exclaimed, "How could you even know that?"

We laughed at a remark that seemed as idle and dangerous as choosing a favorite among one's children.

But my remark was neither idle, nor a choice. I was commenting on the varieties of friendship—that closeness and love are not the same, nor is one necessarily better. They are separate, and different, and equally essential. My comment was one of definition, not hierarchy. I would, in fact, be hard-pressed to pick a favorite child.

Yet because we are all part of some pecking order, it may be inevitable that we try to rank our friendships somehow, to quantify the immeasurable. So, as children, we have lots of "best friends." As teenagers, we discover social friendships. And in adulthood, we can delineate various, more subtle levels of the game.

Still, older friendships have the benefit of history, a saving grace in times when the past is better glue than the present. My oldest friendship, now in its fourth decade, could never have survived without history. I, for one, lost patience for years at a stretch. And yet, with the friendship recently renewed, I am reminded of how history can work, and how deeply it works, like mortar around bricks. Suddenly the gaps dissolve, or they no longer matter. History filled in where the present couldn't provide.

What are we to one another?

We are classmates, confidantes, and golf partners; colleagues, associates, cousins, even. When all is said and done, we are what's there at the beginning and end, when other ties falter or fail, and for everything in between. In the abundant variety of friendship, we are most richly ourselves.

⁓⁓

Serious tea drinkers fall into two groups. In one camp are the purists who relish the act of brewing tea, and the assorted gadgets—tea balls, baskets, strainers—that go along with it. For them, tea is equal parts beverage, process, and ritual.

Then there are those of us who take a low-frills approach, who prefer a cup of loose tea without all the preamble.

Enter the one-cup paper filter.

I happened upon this item several years ago at a coffee shop. Cone-shaped with a flat base, it looked like a small coffee filter. Just fill the bag, brew the tea, and toss it out. Though the process didn't rival the ease of using a standard teabag, the one-cup filter took the ordeal out of brewing loose tea. The real problem was finding more of these elusive filters for home use.

Unable to find a local vendor, I ordered the filters from a manufacturer's website. To my surprise, the Canadian company wanted no payment up front; an invoice would accompany my shipment. At a time when some restaurants require a credit card just to hold reservations, the idea of an online purchase based solely upon trust was a lovely paradox—a digital throwback, at once thoroughly modern and disarmingly quaint. I took an immediate liking to this company that treated customers as if they were neighbors or friends.

My tea filters arrived, along with the bill, a process that would be repeated a number of times over the next few years.

Then last week I received a voicemail message. It was someone named Ted from the tea filter company in Canada, calling with a request. He explained that the firm had mistakenly sent filters to a local ice cream parlor in my area, using regular mail instead of Express Mail.

The shop owner "is in quite a bind and has completely run out of filters," Ted followed up in an email later that day. "The store is located in your zip code, and since you happen to be nearby, we were wondering if you would be kind enough to lend him a package or two. We will then replace whatever you lend and then some."

By any conventional standard, this was an unusual request. After all, what kind of company calls a customer out of the blue, and asks her to lend products to another customer?

Ted's request crossed many lines, not to mention the basic issue of appropriateness. Surely a duplicate shipment of filters, sent for next day delivery, would have solved the problem in a timely, more business-like manner.

But never mind.

This is a company that's willing to ship goods on faith, with no guarantee of payment—and besides, these folks are from Canada. Canadians are notoriously nice. Perhaps they think we are, too.

Frankly, I'm not quite that nice. Ordinarily I would have listened to Ted's phone message, read his email, and deleted both.

But nice begets nice.

From the time of my first online order, I liked this laid-back outfit that freed me from the tyranny of so many tea-brewing devices. Ted's request was so utterly quirky, and yet so strangely inspired, that I decided, against all odds, to go along with it.

Next day, I dropped off several packages of tea filters at the local ice cream shop.

CHAPTER THIRTEEN: THE GREAT OUTDOORS

Still life: empty clothesline, rowboats at water's edge, marsh grasses blowing, but barely.

Almost nothing moves in the still life that is framed by the window of our vacation cottage in Maine. I look for the sly ripple of water, a ruffle of leaves, some sign of motion. But I am the sum total of what is moving.

Of course, there is endless movement in the water—plant life and animals beyond my immediate view. But the window frames what I can see, and the search for movement, for what is there, is altogether too much activity. Watch and listen, the view seems to say; it will compose itself around you.

By the third day, light falls differently on the view framed by the window. And the light falls differently in me. It is Thursday—or Friday, perhaps—but who cares? A sense of timelessness has set in. All days are created equal in this simple, restful place, divided only by sunlight, or rainfall, or nighttime.

To escape the naming of days is the first flush of freedom—to accept that we are meandering and clockless, unbound by time or deadline.

It is approaching midnight. We are at a shoreline dive, eating dinner. We lost track of time, lost time altogether, nearly lost the moment for dinner before breakfast would have rolled around. It is a victory for whatever day it might be.

On the fourth day, I have not tired of the view from the window, yet I am drawn to another pose: the marsh grass to the left, a huge expanse of skeletal, earthen reeds, is entirely different from its counterpart through the window frame. Is it the angle of light, the relation to water, the shape of the grasses themselves?

The grass to the left belongs to another season, it seems; its stark haze resembles winter more than the heart of summer where we sit. And yet to marvel at the disparity between grasses seems over-blown: just observe, and distinguish where there may be a pur-pose. Let the rest go unnamed.

So many days of full, heavy, ponderous sleep bring me to the window this morning half-drunk with restfulness. The view has actually changed. Everything is moving—the rowboats rock in the water, marsh grasses bend at the top, clothespins tremble on the line. I am all that is still.

How did this happen in the space of one week?

There is no drug that can do this, no salve that can unearth the deep calm of a week outside oneself. I am the souvenir that I bring home.

❧ ☙

When we first moved to Maine, I was taken with the view from our deck. Out back, the woods sloped down to a river which, in turn, offered a daily pageant of boats. Starting each spring, a rainbow of kayaks and canoes would glide by, performing a little ballet. The choreography of their passage—short stroke, brief glide, bold slice of color—was one of the reliable beauties of the place.

Or so we thought.

After a couple of years, we noticed fewer boats passing by, even on the best of days. We wondered whether the local boat shop had closed, or whether, perhaps, a recent dredging of the river had halted boating. We theorized all manner of reasons why the boats might recede from our view, but came up empty-handed. For no apparent reason, it seemed, the daily procession had vanished.

Meanwhile, I was starting to find the view from our deck a bit sloppy. While woods aren't generally subject to the same critique as a teenager's bedroom, the term, alas, applied. Our path to the river had melded into its surroundings, leaving us to improvise our way down to the water.

What was once a path had become an article of faith. Ferns

had grown tall, leaves had piled high, and the dense undergrowth had outgrown its rightful place. Looking down toward the river, we could see layers of forest almost without end.

Then it dawned on me: The boat shop hadn't closed, nor was the river off-limits for boating. Nature had simply run its course, growing unattended and taking with it our view. It was entirely possible that the kayaks and canoes were still coasting by each day, masked by our wall of greenery. That was my working theory, at least.

Armed with pruning shears and handsaw, we ventured into the woods. If there was hope for reclaiming our view, some serious maintenance was in order. We hacked away at the underbrush, tamed the ferns, and trimmed branches that had turned gangly. We uncovered a path that had lost all definition and freshened its contours. But the question remained whether so much cleaning could actually bring back the boats.

The joke, it turns out, was on us. We had focused so totally on those boats that we failed to notice the gradual cluttering of our view—a literal case of not seeing the forest for the trees. In fact, the boats had never left. It just took a different vision, and some pruning, to make them reappear.

❧

It was one of those warm summer days that tempts people to leave their desks and lures them outdoors. Fine with me, it seemed, to work in the open air, the breeze as my air conditioning.

What I hadn't factored into the equation, though, was the scene on our deck: flights coming and going all day, boarding from different platforms, for different destinations; fliers pushing, shoving, each trying to get somewhere fast.

In nature's version of an airport, the fliers in question may be winged and small, but they, too, have their priorities. Birds create all that ruckus for a reason. Like us, they're angling for the freshest food, the best perch, a suitable mate.

And who can blame them?

Still, if competing birdcalls, takeoffs, and landings don't get your attention, perhaps the birds' colors will. A pair of goldfinches lands at the bird feeder, their yellow bodies bobbing for food. Try minding your own business when patches of gold flit and dart in front of you.

I quickly realize that the plan to take my work outdoors was naïve, too easily foiled by all of that flapping and chattering. I admit we've compounded the problem by setting out bird feeders and keeping them well-stocked. The birds are indeed welcome, if only we could work out some noise-abatement program.

In its absence, I've taken a different tack. Years ago, when I was new to this front-row viewing of nature, I'd sometimes trot out the binoculars. I had this idea that if sounds in the woods could be matched to their visual counterparts, their pairing might provide some appeasement. So I'd point the binoculars in the direction of the sound, in hopes of a sighting. So rarely did I locate anything resembling a bird that I finally gave up.

The truth, of course, is that the woods are a virtual maze of potential perches, few of them visible from any one spot. With that level of density, even the loudest, most operatic of birds could be hiding in plain sight.

Needle in a haystack, anyone?

Still it takes an act of will to tune out the cacophony of so many birds—and birds are just one of the mouthier species out back. We also have a fair assortment of buzzing, skittering, prancing, leaf-chomping, tree-climbing, scent-spraying wildlife—most of it audible.

So I was surprised recently when guests, sitting in the same outdoor spot, had exactly the opposite response: one of them asked, "Did it take you a while to get used to the quiet?"

◈

Our house offers two distinct vantage points—one side nestles into the woods, another opens to the garden. The two are sufficiently different that guessing the time of day from each, at the same moment, invariably leads to different results. The days appear longer on the garden side, harder to gauge in the woods. A fleeting midday thunderstorm can feign the arrival of nightfall in the woods, whereas the same scenario in the garden arrives with less drama, less chance for deception.

This two-for-one arrangement lends itself to some odd debates. I've come to realize, for instance, that rain in the woods appears to have a longer half-life than it does in fact. Simply put, there are more obstacles to surmount en route to the ground. Each branch, limb, and leaf acts as a temporary way station. Rain doesn't just fall in the woods; it tumbles in stages.

The wind, it turns out, complicates everything. Just when you think the rain has stopped, the wind kicks in to restart the process, or so it seems. What it really incites is a battle of the senses.

Standing by the door to the woods, I can see and hear rain. Looking out at the garden, I see and hear no such thing.

Yet both perceptions are accurate.

It's no longer raining on either side—period. But in the woods, gusts of wind stir up a semblance of rain, which is actually the sound and shimmy of wet leaves shedding water. This defies the quacking duck rule: If it looks like rain, sounds like rain, and acts like rain, it must be rain.

Perhaps "faux rain" would be a fitting concession, allowing for both the fact and the facsimile. Beyond that, the wind sometimes issues a series of postscripts. Hours after a heavy rainfall, a splatter of drops might fall on the deck, seemingly apropos of nothing. It's just the wind loosening more water from the trees. Granted, the entire pattern is familiar, with its own rhythm and sequence. Still, none of that makes the dialogue between wind and rain seem less surprising.

Then there's one final hitch. The skylight facing our woods amplifies everything: Raindrops pound the glass, winds threaten, sounds reverberate. All but the lightest rain mimics a storm.

When an actual rainstorm hits, it might as well be a performance. The skylight is a great contortionist, turning everyday weather into special effects.

∽ֆ ֆ∾

I like my neighbors well enough, though I prefer them when the foliage is full. Not that anything changes between us in winter—we wave and greet each other throughout the year. But in leafless seasons, neighbors are just more apparent. Their comings and goings, cars pulling in and out—all are more obvious.

Come spring, these same neighbors come and go as usual, as do their cars and voices—all pleasantly blurred by an abundance of greenery.

Yet consider the various spectacles that neighbors create. Last winter, I watched a trophy house sprout up around the corner. From week to week, it seemed to gobble up its own land. Then the trees grew fuller as the leaves filled in, and the building receded into the landscape. Now the house is more guesswork than eyesore, small patches of shingle peering through the trees. Is Mother Nature in on this business of neighborliness?

In a good season, foliage even has one up on Robert Frost. Ample leaf cover builds tacit fences without the literal counterparts. It's a six-month reprieve that nature puts up gratis. No need to question what I'm walling in, or walling out, since I'm not *doing* anything. Neighborliness can thrive while nature runs its course.

Nor is foliage merely a visual pacifier. Through layers of green, one can hear the sound of kids and dogs playing in the distance. Or a buzz saw on a Saturday afternoon evoking some home improvement down the road. The audio portion alone is more intriguing. Remember music before music videos?

Which cuts both ways: Just as we were moving in a few years back, a neighbor was moving out. One afternoon, I heard her screaming at her kids in the driveway. I have no idea what provoked her outburst, since my view was blanketed by leaves. Nor did I ever meet this woman, who moved only days later. But I was left with that single jarring impression—a shrewish tone, unseen and unsettling.

Foliage may be a part-time affair in New England, but then, so are the intimations of neighbors.

꧁꧂

It is September and our perennial garden is gorgeous. Not the gorgeous of mid-summer with its dazzle of color, but the dense, quieter beauty of early fall with its abundant textures. The flowers are less vibrant now, less numerous, less everything, if truth be told. What remains—some asters, a butterfly bush, an occasional rose—are like dots on a map, no longer entire regions.

So this is what it's come to: The bustle of summer gardening gives way to an orderliness of greens. All of that cutting back and trimming and staking pays off in multiples—first by blooming, then reblooming, then with foliage that gains stature over time. Come fall, shrubs and bushes take center stage, framed by what the flowers have left behind.

So much for poetry.

This time last year, the same view was a mess. I was new to the garden, indeed new to gardening. True, I had dabbled with houseplants over the years, but nothing that would prepare me for this. Having moved into a new home, I had inherited a full-blown perennial garden. My predecessors, an older English couple, really knew their stuff. No sooner did the snow finish melting than the crocuses would appear, and then the daffodils. The succession of tulips, allium, peonies went on for months as the palette lightened, darkened, and relocated. There was no single theme, color, or height—just an unending variation of elements.

This was a garden designed for the restless eye. And this was my challenge: to ensure that the plantings didn't collapse from the weight of my ignorance.

I scraped by that first season, with no shortage of floundering and a drought, to boot. That most of the garden pulled through intact seemed an improbable victory; the odds for disaster were so obvious. With nature's vote of confidence, I entered the second season less daunted. Armed with pruning shears and puffed up from my early unfounded success, I forged my way through another cycle.

Midway through, it dawned on me that much of gardening is like housework–with a more interesting result. Just as vacuuming removes unwanted groundcover in the home, weeding yields the same effect outdoors. For every cluttered desktop, dusty shelf, or pile of stuff that belongs somewhere else, there is a counterpart in the garden.

Suddenly I was on familiar turf. Guided by a lifetime of domestic caginess, I could apply certain household tricks to the garden. Among them: neatness covers a multitude of sins; apply crowd control, as needed; view everything at a distance.

So I stand by my view of the garden in September. Owing to no particular expertise on my part, it remains gorgeous. I have my predecessors to thank for this, along with the lessons of light housekeeping.

꧁ ꧂

If you watch autumn leaves falling, you'll see a natural ballet. Each leaf moseys to the ground, slow and singular, as if taking in the scenery along the way. From taller trees, the descent seems so long as to be choreographed.

Is it possible that a leaf, left to its own devices, would dawdle like that?

Less choreographed, however, is the aftermath.

Come autumn, all of that leaf fall is the bane of every homeowner. It's one of life's little jokes: the more one rakes, the more leaves there are to rake.

We make countless promises to ourselves every day. We vow, for instance, not to repeat the mistakes our parents made. Or we swear to forgo that daily Dove Bar. Somewhere between the global and the minute are the middling promises that are more like reflexes.

You wake up on a Sunday morning to the blare and fumes of a gas-powered leaf blower, and swear that you'd never assault your neighbors' senses with such a device.

Nor do you mean to lie. But by hour six of raking your own lawn, you've had a change of heart. Surely they make leaf blowers that are less boisterous, kinder on the airways.

And that's what I bought—a sedate electric model, quiet and fumeless, that wouldn't turn me into the enemy. After five hours of use, I can now report that the leaf blower is neither the devil I feared, nor the panacea I'd hoped for. Initially, at least, it's fun—in that new toy sort of way. Then, when the leaves don't visibly recede, the fun does. You've traded the sore back of raking for the sore arms of leaf blowing, with little to show for it.

Alas, sore is sore, whatever the parts.

The leaf blower is satisfying in an illusory way. Unlike raking, with its simple methodical pull, whipping leaves into an autumnal frenzy just *feels* productive. Instead of creating piles of leaves, you can make mounds, borders, and boundaries—a geographical statement, of sorts.

Yet for all that gusto, the machine is a bit of a blowhard. It stirs up leaves, to be sure. But in an age of nanoseconds and microwaves, the leaf blower hardly constitutes a quick fix. What it does instead is speed up the illusion of progress, which, in the end, may be all we really want.

❧ ☙

Camping offers many benefits—the challenge of a new environment, a break from routine, an excuse to make s'mores. This assumes, of course, that one is camping by choice.

Sometimes camping happens.

There we were, returning home from a trip, two days before

Christmas. We unloaded the car, which included a cooler filled with food and drinks. Driving at night, one learns to carry whatever snacks may be needed for the ride.

We arrived home late, hungry, with a simple plan: defrost a few pieces of chicken, bake some potatoes, throw together a salad. But when I reached into the freezer, I found that the chicken had beat me to it. Instead of a frozen block, it was a warm breeding ground—trouble written all over it. Nearby veggies were limp, ice cream had turned to soup. I shut the door and checked the clock on the stove. There were no flashing digits to signal a power outage, only the correct time. The fridge was broken. Which made for an unnaturally warm welcome home.

But this was hardly an emergency. If a refrigerator is doomed to fail, could there be a better time or place? It was, after all, late December in New England—cold is our specialty.

It was in that spirit that we repurposed the cooler from the car and christened it our ad hoc refrigerator. Our "travel food" would become our "real food," and all of it went out on the deck. Nature, at least, would provide proper cooling, even if technology wouldn't.

Next day, Christmas Eve, we dumped the entire contents of the faulty fridge and scoured the insides. We went to the supermarket and stocked up on essentials—milk and butter, cream cheese, eggs, and whatever else might fit in our makeshift ice chest. Having made some calls that morning, we knew there would be no quick fix for our ailing equipment, so we'd better settle into our new program.

It was a bit rustic, this camping out in our own home, but we would make do. Whenever we made coffee, or toast, or pretty much anything, it required a trip outside to the deck, the biggest hardship being that brief encounter with winter.

Meanwhile, you don't realize how many habits need to be revised for such arrangements to succeed. I would hate to count the number of times I grabbed the refrigerator door handle, in hopes of returning cold foods to their proper home. But the warm, motionless air would surprise me every time.

By Christmas morning, we had broadened our horizons, turning an unused room into an impromptu cooling station. Soda and juice, lettuce, tomatoes, and broccoli all huddled next to open windows, sharing the chilly air. Ours was a patchwork system—a deck here, a sill there—that served us well under the circumstances.

Until the storm hit.

A bone-chilling, wind-driven snow was about to hobble our little setup. When we heard the forecast, we retrieved some deck furniture from the basement, and rigged up a pair of tables to shield our supplies. Soon we would be shoveling a path to the cooler, but our stash of food, at least, would be spared.

By Day Four, with a pile of snow on the ground, the novelty was wearing thin. In order to butter a piece of toast, one had to put on a pair of boots and gloves, go to the deck, reclaim the butter, spread it on the toast, return the butter to the cooler, come back inside, and remove one's boots and gloves. This, while trying not to shed snow all over the wood floor.

Dry toast was sounding better by the minute.

And so was a working refrigerator—the conventional kind, with a functioning motor, and all our cold foods in one place.

❧❦❧

Blizzards have much to recommend them. They produce mountains of glistening white snow, school cancellations, and work-at-home days. Yet in these tech-centric times, a blizzard can deal a serious blow to our digital lives, throwing us offline, and generally off. We do what we can to forestall a digital blackout, powering up our devices and stockpiling rechargers. If only we were as realistic in other areas of our lives.

"We have to prepare for a client who's arriving from Italy on Wednesday," a friend protests in the face of a looming storm.

Well, no, your client won't be arriving when flights are cancelled across the board. Score one for the blizzard, zero for those all-important plans.

"I'll pick up a loaf of bread and a gallon of milk on my way home," says the well-meaning spouse, unaware that these mainstays are the holy grail of blizzard shopping, long gone from the store's shelves.

"We have deadlines to meet and meetings to attend, and we're already running behind," says another worker bee, unmoved by the storm. Except that nothing moves in a snowstorm, unless it's a plow, and even that with difficulty.

The beauty of blizzards is the dent they make in our armor, the blow to self-regard, when blowing and drifting snow manages to shut down most worldly ventures. Nor must it be a back-breaker to dole out such insult. Piles of the powdery, nearly weightless stuff bring home the point.

Yet for all the dangers inherent in massive snowstorms, they come with surprising safeguards. For one, fewer fools are out on the roads, and fewer of them are texting. And the ones who are out, are learning how to dance. Major snowfalls demand a new choreography—a sort of two-step for radically reduced roads. The two-way street of other seasons is now a one-lane hazard, and nobody gets to barrel ahead. Each of us has to pull over, allow someone to pass, take turns being polite. It's a mannerly business, this driving on snow-narrowed roads, and a boon to etiquette, as well.

Moreover, blizzards are arguably an old-fashioned, naturally occurring forerunner of Facebook. Friends in warmer parts see and hear the news of our whitened state, and they revel (briefly) in their shovel-free lives. Then their empathy kicks in, and they pick up the phone. Envious they're not, as they'll happily proclaim. At this stage of the season, we're ready to allow that a long-distance strategy for dealing with New England winters has some obvious merit. Tropical island, anyone?

Most of us will welcome an end to winter when it arrives. But a blizzard every now and then is a useful thing, reminding us, as it will, of forces we don't control.

CHAPTER FOURTEEN: SCENTS

I am lying on top of the chemist—twelve feet above him, to be exact. I am asleep in my bedroom, which abuts the kitchen, over his kitchen, where every morning, coffee brews while I sleep. The alarm clock has a prologue: coffee seeps through the walls and floorboards, insinuating itself into my nose.

Among waking sensations, coffee is nearly perfect—pungent, articulate, self-contained. It asks for nothing, wants nothing, and only gives. It is the sort of pleasure that can come only from things, and from the natural world, and so it endears me to the chemist, whom I barely know.

As I start my work day, I am walking on the chemist's head—twelve feet above him. My office sits on top of his office; the rhythms of his work day are as familiar as my own. He is writing a monograph on nitrogen, working for hours at a stretch. At times he is so quiet, and for so long, that the only sign of life below is the hint of coffee pressing up into my apartment. He is now on the second of many coffee cycles, brewing beans in his office, under my desk.

He does not mean to be giving me any particular pleasure; it is the most passive of gifts. But this coffee—all essence and by-product, secondhand scent—has a wonderful irony. Though I no longer drink coffee myself, I still find its moist, acrid smells intoxicating. He is filling a void that began when my java days stopped. He brews, I sniff, we work.

By afternoon, I have added music to the mix. I am listening to Gregorian chant, ancient choral music that loops round and round, entrancing, meditative. To call it hypnotic is, at best, an understatement; it is, arguably, music to sleep by. And it occurs to me that, as the chemist approaches his sixth, or tenth, or twelfth cup of coffee, this music may be just the antidote he needs. This is no decaf I'm smelling; it is unabashed killer brew.

By early evening, I measure the day's work. Then I consider the countless tiny diversions—the pleasures of working at my desk, encircled by the lovely ambient smells. And I factor in the Gregorian chant. All days should be like this, without complaint. Was it good for him, too?

I'll never know, and don't quite care, except perhaps to repay the pleasure. I didn't aim to please him with the music, but would be just as pleased to know I had.

A few hours from now, the entire cycle will begin again: Lying on top of the chemist, twelve feet below, coffee brewing, the day opening before us. It is not just the simple inadvertence of this pleasure that so pleases—though that, too. It is the reminder of how pleasure works in even the smallest ways—coffee brewing, plain chant, ears, nose, senses, alive.

❦

I had just loaded the groceries into my trunk when he walked by. He was combing the parking lot, looking for shopping carts, when he saw mine. We smiled at each other, I handed him the cart. The entire exchange lasted maybe ten seconds. It took me back twenty years.

What happened was this: It was a sweltering summer day. The young man who took my cart was smoking a cigarette. He had just exhaled. The smoke hung in the air, motionless—a cloud framed by heat. And the smell of the smoke hung, as well, with nowhere to go.

Amid the foul city smells that day, cigarette smoke ranked high on the list. And yet I was tempted to linger, like the smoke itself, inhaling its stale, sweet stench. What is it that so tempts even an ex-smoker of long standing?

Instantly, my mind compiled a catalog of cigarettes past: there were the after-dinner smokes whose pleasure exceeded that of most desserts; the cigarettes that bought time and distraction in a heated talk; and the cigarettes that served as punctuation—the pause between thoughts. Cigarettes were an extension of the hand, a tool of the emphatic gesture. So encompassing was the habit that it became nearly inseparable from most activities and things.

To breathe was to smoke.

It is an odd habit, this sucking of dirt, which is what smoking really is. Yet I always envied those whose habit was well-modulated—say, three or four cigarettes a day. It was the golden mean applied to an addiction—a paradox, at best.

For many of us, though, the average was more like twenty, maybe thirty, cigarettes a day, and most of those were smoked so hazily as to go nearly unnoticed. Which is why smokers sometimes have two cigarettes burning at once. It's as if we were smoking in our sleep; we practically were. We acquired smoker's cough and smoker's voice, yellowed fingertips, and rank smoky smells on our clothes. Yet there was that handful of cigarettes each day that somehow justified the rest—small pleasures so complete and self-contained that we couldn't resist.

So this is what we've come to: as former smokers, we inhale the smoke of others, almost pining for the habit we kicked. Indeed, I know an ex-smoker who urges friends to blow their cigarette smoke her way. Proximity is what counts. This way, she gets a whiff of evil on an otherwise virtuous path.

❧ ❧

We hear a lot these days about pork and pork barrels, and not in a good way. The pork in question is all excess and fat, a world apart from the lean and tasty kind. Which brings me to the moment, last week, when my nasal curiosity was piqued.

Standing by a window, I felt the chill of an autumn night, which sometimes reveals what the neighbors are up to. There may be a whiff of woodsmoke in the air, olfactory evidence of the life inside those clapboard homes. But as I inhaled, my brain had trouble decoding the facts. It wasn't a mere smell of bacon; it was a declaration of bacon, bold and concentrated, pouring through my window.

Which neighbor was cooking, I wondered, and how much bacon must it take to gather such a scent?

Bacon, it's said, is a gateway food. It can lead to pepperoni, bacon cheeseburgers, even chocolate.

Yes, for some folks, the combination of bacon and chocolate is heaven. There's a gourmet bacon-and-chocolate bar on the market that ostensibly serves as proof.

Proof of what, you ask? That all roads lead to chocolate, and bacon is a fine way to get there. But I digress.

If you've watched any food shows on television, you know that bacon is an equal opportunity temptation. Chefs, diners, food critics—most admit some degree of weakness for bacon, and in a surprising range of dishes.

Still, the best use of this pedigreed pork may well be the simplest. When the components are right, nothing can beat a basic BLT. Yet too often this venerable sandwich suffers from one or more common defects. Dull, flavorless tomatoes are the standard culprit and the bane of every tomato lover. While heirloom varieties offer some comfort, they're rarely at hand when you need them.

Equally annoying is lettuce that lacks crunch, soggy toast, and inferior mayo. Yet in a single bite, bacon can forgive many of these failings. Bacon is like that. Its sweet smokiness, cushioned among other flavors, saves the day. Nor does it hurt if the aroma lingers in the air while you eat—just another way to infuse several senses at once.

The smoky fragrance that found its way to my window the other night was only part of the story. Between my neighbor's house and mine, the bacon mingled briefly with the tang of autumn leaves.

Mind you, either smell, left to its own devices, would have caught my attention.

Their accidental pairing was irresistible.

❧

Wearing perfume is an art. The fact that women wear it, like gloves or shoes, rather than spraying it randomly into the air, suggests a certain kind of fit. With gloves, for instance, one wants a degree of snugness, comfort, flexibility. "Like a hand in a glove" is the phrase that signifies perfect fit, a metaphor that defies the notion of one-size-fits-all.

So it is with perfume. Mixing bottled and bodily scents does not always add up to the same result. It's an individual response, a certain chemistry that makes one woman's Chanel smell different from another's. Factor in such variables as the weather, the dress one's wearing, and assorted other details, and it seems remarkable that perfumes are identifiable at all. Our very presence adulterates, or at least tempers, a superimposed scent.

So much for moderating influences.

Some women are naturally heavy-handed with an atomizer. Despite the best early training—that perfume is to be strategically placed, a hint here, a dab there, in quantities that imply rather than assert—some women just make up their own rules.

If less is good, then more is better, the logic seems to go. And so there are women, thousands of them, who waft into restaurants, meetings, theaters, and stores, leaving a perfumed trail in their wake. Upholstered chairs absorb the smell from their clothing; the air hangs heavy with their scent.

Perfume isn't contagious, exactly, but it might as well be. When a fragrance attaches itself to the surfaces in a room, it effectively takes over the space.

Did we ask for this?

In fact, it's mostly inadvertent. Over the years, I've polled sever-

SOMEDAY THIS WILL FIT

al of my perfume-wearing friends about their habits. In most cases, they admit to having a weak sense of smell, for which they over-compensate. They apply only as much perfume as needed—that is, whatever it takes to register on their own nasal Richter scales. Never mind that the rest of us are bowled over by the excess.

Nor does the inadvertence stop there. Many allergy sufferers will ask guests to please refrain from wearing perfume when they come to visit. The guests comply, but the improvement is often minimal.

How could this be?

As it turns out, the weak-of-nose also fail to detect perfume residues that linger in their clothes. They may, in fact, not be wearing perfume on a given day, but their suits and coats still wear it from a week before.

Given the unwanted results of too much perfume, certain brand names take on an ironic air. The name "Poison," for instance, is meant to suggest drop-dead appeal, not toxic fumes. Likewise, "Eternity" is meant to confer an aura of unending allure, not some odor that wouldn't give up.

The conventional girlhood lessons about fragrance were right on track: perfume should be subtle, quiet, a small personal pleasure, not a broad-based attack. Though times have changed, and women have gained enormous freedom, there are certain liberties that no woman should ever take.

❦

Some people have a sixth sense. I'm one of them, if you count my nose—twice. Even as a child, I was called upon to assess the fitness of various foods in our house. The milk was either fresh or sour, a stew was beyond its prime, muffins were ready to be tossed. Not that I had mature judgment at the age of six, but I did have an uncanny sense of smell.

Nor is that meant as a boast. I came into the world nasally gift-ed, an accident of birth. This is neither an acquired skill, nor one that garners much reward. Truth is, there are more foul smells than pleasant ones, making a keen sense of smell a mixed blessing. When a scent appeals, the pleasure is greater for those of us able to enjoy it. When an odor is just that, the displeasure is multiplied.

To look at me, one would never know that I possessed this rarified skill. If one imagines a discerning nose to have a certain length and reach, thereby allowing it to take in the full range of scents, mine would go unnoticed. My nose is modest in size, thin and straight—perfectly ordinary in appearance. Whatever it may lack in size or stature, however, it gains in sheer cunning.

I can walk into a building and discern that the walls were recently painted, floors finished, or rugs installed. All that's missing from my assessment are the exact dates. I can sniff out cleaning agents by brand and type, and sense the residues of products that never quite vanished—think moth balls.

While many of these smells are less than attractive, I've come to think of my nasal talent as an early warning system. Certain common fumes and chemicals are problematic for many people. But a simple whiff is all I need to anticipate larger trouble, and to remove myself from the premises.

Similarly, I can detect newly paved roads from afar, a gas leak before it's apparent to others, and countless odd smells before they reach a critical mass. Friends have long marveled at this knack, as if I were prescient; it's my nose that deserves credit. Over the years, I admit to having developed nasal envy: I can only aspire to the track record my nose has achieved.

There is, of course, a downside to this arcane skill. Certain fragrances don't merely waft in my direction; they seem to plant themselves right under my nose. Thus, a flowering Narcissus can seem assaultive; "air fresheners" are anything but; and a cup of tea, brewed too long, can smell and taste like bacon. Such dislocations of scent and sense come with the territory. Taste and smell are inextricably linked. Without a sense of smell, there's little taste. Which still doesn't explain the mystery of coffee, whose flavor can't begin to rival its aroma.

Fortunately, food and nature supply some of the more winning scents, among them apples, cocoa, and bread; autumn leaves, newly-cut grass, and barbecue. While most people can properly identify the smell of an outdoor grill, few mortals can accurately name the food that's cooking.

That's where noses like mine come into play—seasoned, agile, precise, ready for the job at hand.

Is anyone hiring?

CHAPTER FIFTEEN: DEPARTURES

I waited too long. When my laptop computer started to limp a year ago, I decided to hang on. Another year of service was all I asked of it. But over the months, the limp slowed to a crawl and, finally, to a virtual standstill.

"System resources dangerously low," the error message warned.

At the age of four, my computer was conducting its own digital dirge. With its daily jolts and misfires, it fairly begged to be replaced. Dotage in any species is not a pretty sight.

My new laptop offers much in the way of improvement. It's sleek, agile, and muscular—flat-out fast and lighter than its predecessor. As a piece of equipment, it's the perfect slave: responsive and unerring. I command, it performs, and instantly. In the service of so many and wide-ranging tasks, one could hardly ask for more—except, of course, that it have some counterpart in real life.

The saying used to be "All things come to those who wait." That, however, has given way to the more obvious modern truth: crankiness comes to those who wait.

No sooner do we decide to click a certain button, or tap a particular key, than a website appears, or an email flies in from the ether. We now expect each function to occur in some accelerated universe where time exists in perpetual fast-forward. No wonder our patience strains when things take longer than a nanosecond.

(Reality check: Most things do, and always will, take longer than a nanosecond.)

Oddly, "fast foods" have become the common metaphor for the ills of hurrying. But next to the latest tech devices, fast foods could pass for leisurely meals. They take actual minutes to prepare, and can be observed through several stages—frozen, raw, cooked. Compare that to a device whose workings are, at once, invisible, instantaneous, and complete.

Of course, I enjoy the speed and efficiency of my new laptop. What concerns me is the illusion it fosters—that waiting is a curse of incurable slowness, and impatience its due. Beyond the microcosm of this keyboard, in most aspects of life, the exact opposite is true. Waiting is the process that brings about ripening, movement, change. In the natural course of events, time needs simply to elapse. But try convincing young people of that, when they spend hours every day in front of a screen.

More to the point, try convincing your own grownup psyche, after a day when your mobile gadgets are fast, flawless, and wait for nothing.

When I think back to my former laptop, with its hesitations and double takes, there's something strangely comforting in its tentative ways. An old, outdated device is the very essence of waiting, almost to the point of parable. It offers more of a lesson than we bargained for. As a model for humans, though, it remains truer and more lifelike than its pumped-up protégés.

❧❧

It is simply a fact that we can never get inside another person's mind. Try as we may to grasp another's thoughts, or motives, or point of view, we are always working at a disadvantage.

It is their world, not ours.

Entire professions exist purely to solve some of the thornier mysteries afoot—how an accident happened, why a crime was committed, how some seemingly inexplicable thing can be explained. When a plane crashes or a bomb explodes, investigators can reconstruct the physical parts to simulate the event. By examining the evidence, its scars and markings, some logic might emerge. So, too, with crime scenes. Detectives replay a scenario from various angles that could reasonably produce the evidence they found. They hope to grasp the pilot's, perpetrator's, or victim's state of mind. They try to inhabit another person's brain.

If there's one lesson to be learned from these efforts, it is about the limits of human knowledge: we know so little about most things, and what we do know is invariably a blend of fact, speculation, and theory. Above all, we have a need to put a lid on endless wondering. It's what we've come to call "closure." At some point, we'll settle for any answers—even false ones—rather than accept the prospect of no answer at all. It is a humbling thing, all of this not knowing.

It is a year now since my friend Richard died, give or take a few days. Those extra days allow for a certain miscalculation—the difference between when the police found his body rotting inside the house, and the day when his heart actually gave out. This small mathematical fact, the lack of an exact date of death, should have been ample warning. There would be few facts uncovered, just countless uncertainties.

The absence of facts only furthered the need for answers—to search, reconstruct, try to fathom why, at forty-five, Richard took his own life. Without any note or specific clues, he left only a vague trail of evidence—unpaid bills, empty gin bottles, filth everywhere. One could piece together a semblance of the physical process at hand. But to trace the inner process that led Richard to this state, one can only guess.

A year ago, when it happened, I thought I understood Richard's death, if only in some small way. Not that I presumed to understand more than I could; but the weight of not knowing was too great. Like other of his friends and family, I invented ways to grapple with his death. I combined hard facts with half-truths in search of some workable blend of painkillers. Which is exactly the point: we invent answers and explanations in order to dull the pain.

When people wonder why we continue to explore how the world came into being, I think we are always circling the same territory. We need to know something, and that need itself is far greater than any facts we'll ever know. That may explain our readiness to accept certain theories at a given time, and to dismiss them when something better comes along. We can only tolerate so much not knowing.

Looking into the endless void may well be the preface to all invention. We invent answers, theories, even reasons for life and death. It is necessity mothering itself.

❧❧

My brother Steve was forty when he finally won custody of his teenage son. After years of legal wrangling, the victory came as a huge relief. Steve was convinced that my mother knew in advance of the verdict, and was somehow behind it; she should, therefore, be the first to know.

Unable to reach her, he wrote a note and delivered it in person. He went to the cemetery and wedged the tightly folded piece of paper between the earth and my mother's grave.

"You did *what?*" I said in disbelief.

He repeated the words, as if the repetition would somehow explain the obvious logic of his action. I could grasp the note-writing part; actually delivering it left me speechless.

During the following years, Steve and I had other exchanges in which he ruminated aloud. "I had a talk with Mom today," he would say, despite the fact that my mother had died several years before. Or "Mom liked the new house we rented," as if my mother were there to appreciate it.

I never questioned Steve about these dissonant, odd phrasings, and almost got used to hearing them. The lack of questioning was not, however, due to any lack of curiosity. I was extremely curious about Steve's view of the world, and my mother's apparent presence in it. But the fact that we were talking about the same mother could not override my sense that Steve was describing something completely private, between my mother and him, outside of me. That he had given her an afterlife, an existence beyond death, was part of it. But the sheer defiance of reinventing my mother in the present tense left me speechless. Which is, perhaps, as it should be.

Unlike virtually anything else, one's memories of someone who has died are entirely singular. Conversation on the subject is by invitation only. I should have learned this from my mother when she was dying.

During the three months of her illness, my mother spoke often about death, about her belief in an afterlife, and about her own mother's death. She would describe an afterlife in vivid, compelling terms as if it were a travel destination. In a sense, I suppose it is.

She also recalled this story. About a year after her own mother had died, my mother, then thirty, had a strange experience. She was asleep one winter night, the blankets half-tossed off the bed. She awoke to the sensation of her own mother pulling the blankets over her shoulders, under her chin. My mother's telling of the story was a simple relating of facts, unembellished.

I don't know what actually occurred that night. My mother's story seemed so complete, so self-contained, that it left no room for inquiry. To question it would have risked the appearance of a challenge, and the risk wasn't worth it. The closest I ever got to a question was an awkward, self-conscious, "So I might hear from you, or see you, later?"

She nodded, and we moved on to something else.

It is now many years since my mother died, and I have long since given up thinking that I might have my own version of the blanket episode. But years later, I am certain that my mother's "encounter" with her own mother was real. It wasn't an actual physical encounter; clearly, my grandmother was unavailable for blanket tucking. But something happened that night with the blanket that was soothing and sustaining, even if only in a dream. It stayed with my mother for the remaining four decades of her life.

So, what do I make of blankets that get mysteriously tucked in the night, and notes delivered to a cemetery?

I was invited into these conversations to listen; my opinion wasn't sought or desired. It frankly didn't matter. What matters is that even the congenitally curious, like myself, can easily grasp that some kinds of truth are better left unquestioned.

❧❧

I lead a busy life. Last Saturday I attended a wedding at a Baptist church down south, where I chatted up Johnny Carson sitting beside me. We traded Hollywood gossip. Directly in front of me was the very bald pate of Don Rickles, who slept through the whole affair. A gospel choir was led by Bill Clinton, whose conducting skills left something to be desired. In place of the usual arm motions, he kept mouthing the words, "Keep it simple, keep it simple," which they did.

The next day I joined a cult. I have no idea what beliefs its members held, but their outfits caught my eye. They wore Hare Krishna-style robes, of a sturdy fabric, nicely fitted. The color was a rich medium blue, reminiscent of our old high school gym suits. I signed over my earthly goods to the cult in exchange for the robes. I also agreed to occasional dishwashing. Seems that the group was big on baking fresh cakes and pies. They would bake, I would clean.

On Monday I flew to Singapore on business, a bit rushed since I also had to be in New York for a performance of *Rent*. That is, I was performing in *Rent*. No matter that I'd never rehearsed a line or sung a note. The show must go on.

This is but a sampling of the vivid nightlife I've been leading of late, courtesy of REM sleep. These dreams may fill all of five minutes in real time. But they sometimes present day-long puzzles to solve in my waking hours.

What's notable about these dreams is their proximity to real life. Each dream takes some snippet of fact and rearranges it. Take the gospel choir at the wedding. For days now, I've been humming the new television jingle for a certain restaurant chain. It is a feast of gospel-inspired harmony, sung by a group of spirited chefs cooking up a storm. Reality is just the raw material; like clay, it can be stretched and molded into whatever form the brain decides.

The presence of Bill Clinton in the dream is like many of the details—a spin-off of data absorbed from television news just before bedtime. The mind is good at reassembling endless dots and pixels for our amusement. So I combine a Clinton speech, film footage of Johnny Carson, an ad for Singapore Airlines, and the soundtrack to *Rent*. I throw in a few pressures from my daily life and—voila!—it's no longer a single newscast with a sales pitch: it's an entire dream cycle.

Never mind that Clinton is shorthanded in the art of "conducting," or that the cult I join appears to have only culinary goals. As dreamers, we have poetic license.

Dreams, no doubt, serve countless functions. Conflicts can be recast in a fresh format, considered in a new light. By distorting the facts, they can disguise truths that might otherwise be difficult to bear. Dreams are the mind's recycle bin, a place for the day's bit players to gather again and perform. The nightly show is spectacular, in its way, because we accept the unabridged ramblings of the mind at rest.

There's no need to censor; we have our waking lives for that.

※⁂※

Sometimes you see something without really knowing what it is.

Yesterday, for instance, I was leaving my dentist's office. I entered a hallway and headed toward the elevator. At the other end of the hall, I noticed an old man hunched over a cane. I couldn't see his face, just the arc of his back, like an apostrophe. When I looked again, he appeared to be asleep, leaning against a wall, propped up on that cane.

But he wasn't moving. At all.

As I approached the elevator, I wondered whether I was witnessing an ad hoc response to fatigue, a sort of sleeping in place.

I wondered if, in his younger days, he was one of those men you see in stores, sitting with a woman's handbag, snoozing, while his wife is busy shopping. Sleeping is, at bottom, the ultimate show of detachment. Still, the standing part had me stumped. How tired must one be to fall asleep standing? And why wasn't this stooped and fragile man, sandwiched between a wall and a cane, falling over? The sheer physics of the scene made no sense.

Then it dawned on me that something else might be going on here, and maybe I should do something, or notify someone. Before getting on the elevator, I needed to determine whether he was still among us.

So I cleared my throat emphatically, as a kind of test. On the one hand, I didn't really want to disturb him—more power to anyone who can catnap so providentially. On the other hand, disturbing him in some small, unremarkable way was precisely my goal.

My cough didn't have the impact of, say, water on a wilted plant, its stems and leaves visibly swelling. But some part of the hunched figure down the hall shifted, ever so slightly.

Feeling relieved, if somewhat foolish, I boarded the elevator.

❧ ❧

Psychologists are forever trying to explore the depths of human emotion. They want to know our deepest wishes, hopes, and fears. Sometimes, though, our wishes are neither deep nor complicated, but simple longings to return to an earlier state. In the case of women, that state can best be summed up in four words: someday this will fit.

This distinctly female mantra isn't entirely foolish, just largely so. We assume, first off, that the clothes we store will somehow wait for us—that when we return, often years later, the low-slung hips or flared legs of our slacks won't look archaic or quaint. We assume the rights to these clothes, as if to earlier versions of ourselves.

Then we engage in a sort of fashion math: reach a certain weight and, ipso facto, certain clothes will fit. They did, therefore they will. Never mind that our equation permits none of the variables that reality has been known to impose.

Among the surprises: gaining or losing weight is never the same thing twice. We may have notions about how the weight will sit and where it should go. One quickly learns, however, that the body, too, has a plan, which may, or may not, coincide with our own.

Nor does a precedent, set years before, necessarily hold much clout. Unlike memory fabrics that revert to their original shape, bodies have a different, more canny sort of memory. They've put up with us all these years; in turn, they manage to keep us honest. If you're no longer twenty-two, chances are your body won't pretend that you are.

Through some twisted calculus, the business of clothing sizes becomes increasingly surreal with time. That little black dress in the closet, for instance, used to fit well in all the right places. A decade later, you may be the identical weight, but parts of you and the dress are now in different time zones.

What's wrong with this picture?

Nothing, probably. It's just that we hold certain fanciful ideas that morph into expectations. All of those neat assumptions about weight and size, which form the rationale for so many bags of stored clothes, fall apart without adjusting for age. Middle age is a great rearranger of assets; it's the wild card that no simple math can explain.

It should come as no surprise, then, that a middle-aged body has a structure and form distinct from that of its younger self. If that means an entire history of wardrobes past will sit in bags, in the closet, then so be it.

"Someday this will fit" isn't a lie, exactly. It's more complicated than that. Factor in a dose of realism and a sense of humor and, with luck, one learns the difference between what's fitting and what fits.

ACKNOWLEDGMENTS

It really does take a village to make a book. For those of us coming from the newspaper world, book publishing appears to be a close cousin. But one quickly learns that assumption is wrong. Different rules, different game, different everything. And, thus, a major learning curve. For these reasons and more, I am indebted to a number of people.

For providing an overview of the book publishing world, plus the tools and structure to navigate it, I'd like to thank Katrin Schumann. Ellen Cooney supplied helpful critique and cheerleading along the way. Elizabeth Searle offered countless useful pointers.

Two early readers, Betsey Henkels and Candace Platz, were instrumental in determining the final shape of this book.

A shout-out to the late great Joe Shea, who opened a door to essay writing, at a time when I'd grown restless as a features writer.

And nods to several others—Rick Holmes, Sally Heinemann, Bob Davis, David Langworthy—who kept that door open.

A book manuscript is a bare-bones sort of affair, words on a page, in need of shelter and context, a road into the world. The folks at Bauhan Publishing—Sarah Bauhan, Mary Ann Faughnan, Henry James, and Jocelyn Lovering—provided all of that. They have been lovely partners in this project.

And, finally, my thanks to G., for everything.